SYMBOLS OF
ISLAM

Assouline Publishing
601 West 26th Street,
New York, NY 10001
www.assouline.com

© 2000 Assouline Publishing for the present edition
First published in French by Editions Assouline
Les Symboles de l'islam © 1997, 1999 Editions Assouline

Distributed in all countries, excluding France,
Belgium, Luxemburg, USA and Canada,
by Thames and Hudson Ltd (Distributors), London

ISBN: 2 84323 199 X

Translated by Cybele Hay

Printed in Italy

SYMBOLS OF
ISLAM

Malek Chebel

Photographs by Laziz Hamani

ASSOULINE

CONTENTS

"IN THE NAME OF GOD,
THE COMPASSIONATE,
THE MERCIFUL"

PRAISE BE TO GOD,
LORD OF THE WORLDS!
THE COMPASSIONATE,
THE MERCIFUL!
KING ON THE DAY OF RECKONING!

THEE ONLY DO WE WORSHIP,
AND TO THEE
DO WE CRY FOR HELP.

GUIDE THOU US ON THE STRAIGHT PATH,
THE PATH OF THOSE
TO WHOM THOU HAST BEEN GRACIOUS;
– WITH WHOM THOU ART NOT ANGRY,
AND WHO GO NOT ASTRAY.

Al-Fatihah, the first sura of the Koran[1]

1.   Translation by J. M. Rodwell. Everyman's Library: London, 1909.

INTRODUCTION

I. THE BACKGROUND OF ISLAM

Born in the seventh century A.D. in Arabia, Islam is a monotheistic religion focusing on the glorification of the One Supreme Being, Allah, and around a Holy Book, the Qur'an (Koran), revealed between 610 and 623 A.D. to the Prophet Muhammad. Islam was founded at a time when moral and spiritual laxity was at its height in the region of Mecca, further north in Medina, and in the surrounding area.

The fledgling religion was speedily organised around three focal points, Allah, Muhammad and the Qur'an, linked by a single overwhelming message, the constant call to faith and its corollary, the punishment in hell awaiting polytheists, idolaters and miscreants.

In those days, Arabia itself, the "cradle of Islam", and particularly the western region called Hijaz, situated between Mecca and Medina, was idolatrous. Various divinities were worshipped, ten of whom are referred to in the Qur'an: al-Lat, al-Uzza, Manât, Wadd, Suwa, 'Yaghut, Ya'uq, Nasr, Hubal and Taghut.

The Qur'an continuously refers to this initial situation, thus giving Muslim historians through the ages the means to extol the inflexibility of Islam in the face of heresy in all its forms, schism, associationism and various deviations … At the heart of this system of impiety lay Mecca. An important city even then, Mecca was a busy centre of pre-Islamic pilgrimage, which had two main assets:

— a geographical position which made it a necessary stop on the caravan route, a vital link between the south of the peninsula, itself very prosperous, and the northern regions of Syria, Palestine, Egypt and Iraq;

— an active political life and a seasonal assembly point for all the tribes of the peninsula. It was their literary congress and a place where large poetry contests were held.

All these elements were consequently combined to designate this place of impiety as a hotbed of ignorance and irreligion, while its inhabitants were pilloried, *ipso facto*, as blasphemers and "hypocrites" (*munafiqûn*).

Subsequent Muslim orthodoxy has, moreover, spared no efforts in charging this undoubtedly idolatrous population with a multitude of failings, foremost among them that of combating and persecuting the Prophet Muhammad when he began his preaching.

It is from these difficult times that Islam draws virtually all its guiding principles, its ethics and its enduring vigour.

II. THE QUR'AN, ISLAM AND MUSLIMS

Islamic angelology places the Archangel Gabriel in the enviable position of being the herald of the "Glad Tidings", the Qur'an, which the Prophet is merely reciting (*iqra'*) to his disciples in a "perspicuous [clear] tongue".[1] The Qur'an deals with most of the spiritual and moral issues encountered by a

Muslim in his life. This life is considered a transitory state and a precious gift from the Creator.

The Qur'an is a rich and complex text, at once the comforting breviary on which the *imam* meditates, the theological and moral corpus commented on by the scholar, and the sum of spirituality which inspires the Sufi mystic. Muslim jurisprudence is ordered by an imposing set of canonical texts, sometimes going as far back as the origins of Islam, which constitute the *sunna*, the "trodden path" (i.e., by the Prophet). Religious law, called the *shari'â*, flows directly from it and is wholly inspired by it, sometimes in complicated detail. It is still imposed by the governments of several theocracies, such as the Sudan.

The Qur'an's unifying dimension and its structure make it an inimitable text (*i'jâz*). As such, it is truly a "challenge" to the human conscience, an aesthetic entirely apart, surpassing all others in beauty and balance. The meaning of the word *Islam* is a complex one. Its origin is the root s-l-m, which literally means "tranquillity", "peace" (*salâm*), or possibly "to be safe and sound", "to remain whole".

As for the term *aslama*, which means "to submit oneself with complete peace of mind", "to give oneself up to God", it is from this root that the word *Muslim* is derived. Since the believer considers himself to be a servant of God, his obedience is completely His.

Obedience to Allah is one of the key concepts in Islam, because it breaks with the logic of splinter factions and intense rivalry which characterised the pagan polytheism of the Meccans. "Those who obey Allah and His Messenger will be admitted to Gardens with rivers flowing beneath, to abide therein forever and that will be the supreme achievement. But those who disobey Allah and His Messenger and transgress His limits will be admitted to a fire, to abide therein: and they shall have a humiliating punishment"(The Women, IV, 13–14).[2]

The role of the Qur'an also extends to the organisation of temporal life. In regulating an Islamic community which is "the best of peoples, evolved for mankind" (Al 'Imran, III, 110), and which now extends to the ends of the earth, the Qur'an has become a constitution which has been widely tested and which, as has recently been seen, is of a formidable efficacy.

The prevailing union in Islam between the temporal and the spiritual led Muslim theologians, in the period of dynastic greatness, to extend this idea of obedience to the political conduct of the Muslim masses, who thus became not only believers, but also the subjects of the Caliphate. The originality of this new preaching stems from its Arab Bedouin hallmark and the indelible imprint of the founding myths of the Arabian peninsula, as well as the abolition of pagan illusions.

Islam is a sober religion, an aggressive religion, but one that fervently advocates the spiritual equality of all men. It was immediately and definitively organised around five duties which each and every Muslim must observe: the profession of faith, prayer, almsgiving, fasting and pilgrimage to Mecca. These are, however, only the "pillars" (*arkân*) of the dogma and cannot be substituted for the real soul of the "beautiful habitation" which is faith, *al-imân*.

For Muslims, each of the prophets came to liberate a particular people, whereas Muhammad, the last messenger, is the one who addresses the whole of humankind. That being the case, Muslim egalitarianism is amply justified and illustrated. Is it not said in this religion, and in the collective culture born therefrom, that in the sight of God no distinction exists between man and woman or between Arab and non-Arab, except the sincerity of their faith, which alone can decide between them? Moreover, how could a religion which is universal in character be bound by accidents of social origin, fortune or skin colour?

Thus, if the Qur'an represents the Uncreated and Omnipotent Word of the living God, the vocation of Islam is to take its place within the continuation of the Abrahamic tradition, which Arabia, by its proximity, its filiation and its intermingling of populations, furthered and allowed to flourish.

The original Muslim mission lasted for twenty-two years. It began *circa* 610 and ended in June 632. Today Islam raises its standard over a territory stretching from the Atlantic in the extreme north-west of Africa to south-east Asia, via the islands of the Indian Ocean, part of the Balkans and several republics of Central Asia. Egypt, the Maghreb, Turkey, Persia and all the countries of the present-day Near East were Islamicised in the course of the seventh and eighth centuries.

This first period of conversion to Islam was achieved by the sword after the conquest of Andalusia which began in 711. According to the testimony of the Muslims of the classical age (tenth to twelfth centuries), Andalusia was the "pearl" of the *Dâr al-Islam* (the Abode of the Faith) at its height.

The other Muslim regions, sub-Saharan Africa and southern Asia in particular, were converted through the means of *jihad* (Holy War). They were acquired by Islam during a "second mission" which lasted right up to the end of the seventeenth century.

Nowadays, Muslims form the majority in over thirty-five countries and number just under one billion souls worldwide. Western Europe has about seven million Muslims, mainly from the former colonies. Of these, six million live in the three central countries alone: France (three million), Germany (two million) and the United Kingdom (one million).

How can one evoke the images and objects which are associated with Islam, since the sobriety of its rituals, the absence of all ceremony and the systematic refusal to attribute liturgical tonality to objects or garments distinguish it from all other faiths? Islam has no chalice, no host, not even holy water or aspersion. Confession is a concept alien to Islam, and contact with God is made without the aid of intercessors or communion. Moreover, the liturgical symbol of congregation is reduced to its simplest expression: removing one's footwear, reciting the *basmala* and the *shahada*, performing one's ablutions and sitting in a small chapel or mosque are all that is needed to establish direct contact with Allah. For the sincere Muslim, spiritual self-improvement and the deepening of knowledge are of paramount importance. The Prophet himself always set the perfect example throughout his life.

However, Islam cannot long remain outside the field of symbolism, just as it cannot remain insensitive to representation nor detach itself from expressions of beauty and usefulness. For all that, since it is a religion which does not allow for mediation between the Creator and the believer and does not hold with intermediaries, a religion without clergy or icons, let alone idols, the images of Islam are quite distinct from those of other faiths.

III. ISLAM AND OTHER RELIGIONS

Islam recognises the two other revealed religions, Judaism and Christianity, and accords them a special place. Jews and Christians are called "the People of the Book" (*Ahl al-Kitab*), since the law they share is also laid down in a revealed Book: "Say: 'We believe in Allah, and in what has been revealed to us and what was revealed to Abraham, Isma'il, Isaac, Jacob, and the Tribes, and in the Books given to Moses, Jesus and the Prophets, from their Lord. We make no distinction between one and another among them, and to Allah do we bow our will" (The Family of 'Imran, III, 84).

Faithful to biblical teaching, the Qur'an acknowledges the existence of heaven, hell and the Day of Resurrection. It accords a superior status to the angels, recognises the existence of Satan, the Devil, and confirms the punishments which await infidels in the hereafter. As a religion of forgiveness, Islam assures those who recognise the error of their ways that they can expect boundless salvation, since God alone is the guarantor and protector of the believer.[3]

From the beginning, the history of Islam has been a turbulent one, but one that is little known by the outside world. This lack of knowledge is not sufficient in itself to explain the proliferation of writings which have been appearing in bookshops over the last few years. The reason for the curiosity of the neophyte, here exalting the ardour of the Muslim soul weary of material comfort, there reinforcing the faith of the underprivileged, must surely lie elsewhere.

The present work seeks to set out the basic aspects of dogma relating to the doctrine: the profession of faith, prayer, almsgiving, fasting and pilgrimage, as well as familiar aspects of the practice of Islam such as sacrificial rites, the prayer beads, the dress code and the architecture of the buildings in which the faithful congregate—the mosque, the Kaaba, Mecca, the *madrassa*, etc. It seeks to be a visual synthesis of Islamic civilisation at its peak, and, as far as it is able, a living reminder of Islam today.

1. "Verily this is a Revelation from the Lord of the Worlds [...] in the perspicuous Arabic tongue" (The Poets, XXVI, 195).
2. Unless otherwise indicated, excerpts from the Qur'an have been taken from *The Meaning of the Holy Qur'an* by 'Abdullah Yusuf 'Ali (Amana Publications, 1995).
3. "Put thy trust in Allah, and enough is Allah as a disposer of affairs" (The Women, IV, 81).

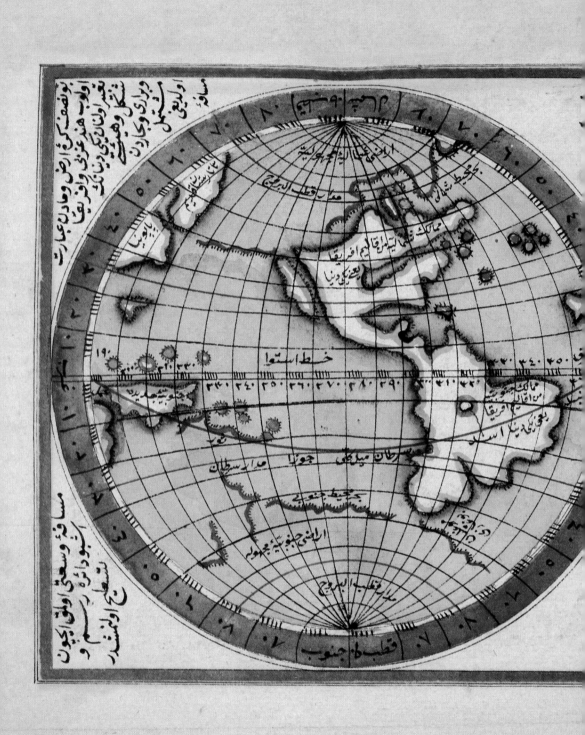

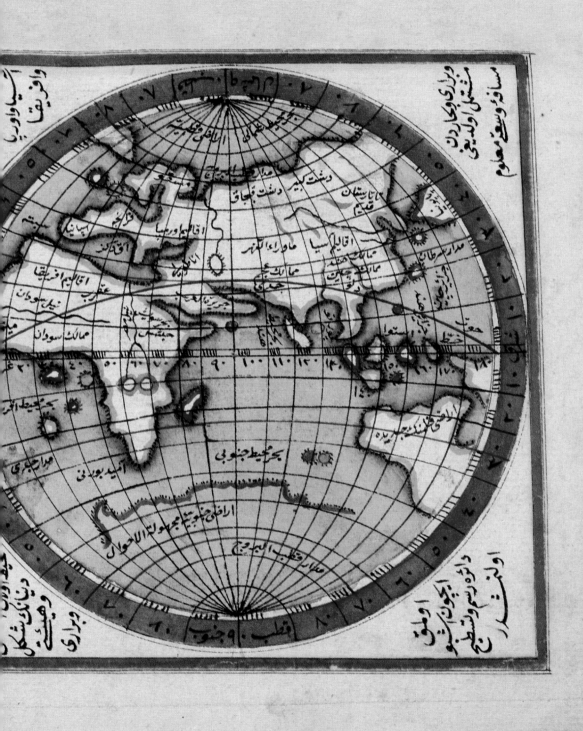

CHAPTER 1

ALLAH

AL-LAH, AL-ILAH, AR-RAB,
DIFFERENT NAMES FOR THE ONE GOD OF ISLAM

IN THE ISLAMIC CONSCIOUSNESS, ALLAH IS THE CREATOR OF THE WORLD AND THE PRIME MOTIVATOR OF ITS WORKINGS. As the God of monotheism, there are two thousand seven hundred references to Him in the Qur'an: "Say: He is Allah, the One and Only; Allah ... the Absolute. He begetteth not, nor is He begotten; and there is none like unto Him" (The Purity of Faith, CXII, 1–4).

Historically, the notion of *Al-Ilah* ("God"), as He is called throughout the Semitic world, existed in the Meccan pantheon long before Islam, but He certainly did not occupy the place He was to take in the Muhammadan mission. The Qur'an reinforces and hallows His primacy and excellence. The omnipotence of Allah (an idea referred to in no less than one hundred and forty-two verses) and His mercy (evoked in one hundred and ninety-four verses spread over seventy-two suras) eclipsed the peninsula's other gods.

How is Allah presented in the Qur'an? This is an important question since Islam is defined both by its radical break with the pre-Islamic pantheon and its vision of the future. The afterlife and the resurrection of the dead are both involved. The Qur'an and the traditions accept the existence of a final day of judgement when evildoers will be punished. Just as they are deciding factors in Judaism, heaven and hell are fundamental facts in Islamic escatology and thought.

The Qur'an abounds in definitions of God. One of the most mysterious and poetic is the definition in the twenty-fourth sura, which states: "Allah is the Light of the heavens and the earth. The parable of His light is as if there were a Niche and within it a Lamp: the Lamp enclosed in Glass; the glass as it were a brilliant star: lit from a blessed Tree, an Olive, neither of the East nor of the West, Whose Oil is well-nigh Luminous, though Fire scarce touched it: Light upon Light!" (The Light, XXIV, 35).

Transcendent and omniscient, knowing all at every moment, Allah is both the guardian and the guarantor of leniency, of clemency (or forgiveness, *ghufrân*) and of mercy, as illustrated by this passage: "Allah is He, than Whom there is no other god— Who knows all things both secret and open; He, Most Gracious, Most Merciful. Allah is He, than Whom there is no other god—the Sovereign, the Holy One, the Source of Peace and Perfection, the Guardian of Faith, the Preserver of Safety, the Exalted in Might, the Irresistible, the Supreme; Glory to Allah! High is He above the partners they attribute to Him. He is Allah, the Creator,

Calligraphy of the name of Allah in the Paris Mosque.

the Evolver, the Bestower of Forms. To Him belong the Most Beautiful Names: whatever is in the heavens and on the earth doth declare His Praises and Glory: And He is the Exalted in Might, the Wise" (The Mustering, LIX, 22–24).

The ninety-nine names of God evoked in these verses are intended to purify the souls of pious women and men and keep them away from the devil.

Their recitation, which is recommended in the Qur'an, is accorded an important place in meditation, especially by the mystics. At all times, in all places, they preserve the believer from evil by keeping it at bay. Seven names have a particularly evocative symbolism: Allah, *Huwa*: "He"; *Al-Haqq*: "The Truth"; *Al-Hayy*: "The Living"; *Al-Qayyum*: "The Subsistent"; *Al-Qahhar*: "The Invincible, the Victorious" and *Al-Rabb*: "The Lord". But the following titles are also common: *Al-Rahman*, "The Merciful"; *Al-Rahim*, "The Compassionate"; *Al-Karim*, "The Most Noble"; and *Al-Tawwab*, which means: "He Who is near to His Creation (*tâb*)". Finally, in the last category of names of God, the faithful tell several attributes of Allah on the prayer beads: *Al-Wahab*, "The Generous Giver"; *Al-Majid*, "The Glorious"; *Al-Fattah*, "The Opener"; *Al-Razzaq*, "The Dispenser of Riches", and so on. On this subject, Ibn-'Abbas recounts hearing the Prophet say: "God has ninety-nine names or one hundred minus one; he who memorises them will enter into Paradise."[1]

The foremost quality of God in the eyes of Muslims is His goodness and His love. God is love.

God is good. God is compassionate. These are the attributes to which the Qur'an and the Prophet refer to the most. Allah is the Giver (*Al-Muâz*), He Who answers the needs of mankind (*Al-Razzaq*).

Expressions such as: "Allah is most surely full of kindness, Most Merciful" (*inna Allaha lara'ufun rahimun*) (The Cow, II, 143) or "My Lord is ... full of mercy and lovingkindness" (*inna rabbi rahimun wadudun*) (Hud, XI, 90), punctuate a great many suras in which Divine Charity has already been mentioned. While the Qur'an is entirely devoted to the greatness and sovereignty of Allah (*jalalâti Allah wa 'udhmatihi*), as well as to His wrath (*ghadâbihi*), the oral tradition of the Prophet enumerates and dissects one by one each of the characteristics of His Majesty, among them "Nearness" (*al-qurb*), which remains one of the most poignant measurements of Islam's intrinsic humanity.

Very little has been explicitly stated about the distance between the believers and God in paradise. There are, however, some testimonies which hint at this, such as the following. According to Jarîr ben 'Abdallah, a Muslim living in the seventh century, the Prophet is reported to have told some people who had gathered around him one night of the full moon: "You will see the Lord even as you see that moon, without having to jostle each other in order to see," and again, from the same witness, "You will see the Lord with your own eyes."[2]

The formula by which God is invoked to bestow His benediction is called the *basmalla*: "In the name of God, (the) Merciful, (the) Compassionate" (*Bismillah al-Rahman al-Rahim*). All the suras of the Qur'an, except the ninth, begin with the *basmala*. Unlike the "good intention" (*niyya*), which is a private thought, the *basmala* is a formula which is spoken or written. Its importance is such that the Prophet said: "All that is in the Revealed Books is contained in the Qur'an, all that is in the Qur'an is contained in the opening sura (*fatiha*), all that is in the *fatiha* is contained in the *basmala*."[3]

During the *basmala*, the following phrase, "Praise be to Allah" (*al-Hamduli'llah*) is used to pay homage to God. It is a phrase which children learn from their earliest days. After each meal they say it in unison, as an expression of their contentment, just as they say the *basmala*. Expressions such as *Subhan'allah* ("Glory to God") or *Istaghfiru'llah* ("I ask forgiveness of God") punctuate a large number of the actions of daily life.

The present list of the ninety-nine names has gradually been superimposed over concurrent lists containing thirty-six, seventy-two or five hundred names. It is estimated that a secret name, the hundredth, reserved for the Prophet and for men of religious insight, completes this prestigious collection.

Apart from these divine names and that of the Prophet Muhammad, the names of the first four Caliphs, called the "Properly Guided Caliphs" (*al-Khulafa' al-Rashidun*), because they, too, are models of virtue, are held in very high esteem: Abu Bakr (d. 634), 'Umar (d. 644), Uthman (d. 656) and 'Ali (d. 661). The same is true of Khadija and 'A'isha, the wives of the Prophet, as well as of His daughter Fatima, the wife of 'Ali. These "beauteous names" inspire Muslims when naming their children. They add the prefix *'abd* (servant) for boys, to give, for example, 'Abd al-Wahab (literally, "The Servant of the Giver").

Female first names are constructed on the same roots, although without prefixes: Rahima, Malika, Karima, etc.

1. *Hadith* of the Prophet.
2. El-Bokhari, *Les Traditions islamiques*, vol. 4, p. 598. (Paris: Maisonneuve et Larose, 1984).
3. *Hadith* of the Prophet.

الْبَاعِثُ ۞ الشَّهِيدُ ۞ الْحَقُّ

الْوَكِيلُ ۞ الْقَوِيُّ ۞ الْمَتِينُ

الْوَلِيُّ ۞ الْحَمِيدُ ۞ الْمُحْصِي

الْمُبْدِئُ ۞ الْمُعِيدُ ۞ الْمُحْيِي

الْمُمِيتُ ۞ الْحَيُّ ۞ الْقَيُّومُ

الْوَاجِدُ ۞ الْمَاجِدُ ۞ الْأَحَدُ

الصَّمَدُ ۞ الْقَادِرُ ۞ الْمُقْتَدِرُ

الْمُقَدِّمُ ۞ الْمُؤَخِّرُ ۞ الْأَوَّلُ

الْآخِرُ ۞ الظَّاهِرُ ۞ الْبَاطِنُ

اَلْمُعِزُّ ۞ اَلرَّافِعُ ۞ اَلْخَافِضُ ۞

اَلْبَصِيرُ ۞ اَلسَّمِيعُ ۞ اَلْمُذِلُّ ۞

اَللَّطِيفُ ۞ اَلْعَدْلُ ۞ اَلْحَكَمُ ۞

اَلْعَظِيمُ ۞ اَلْحَلِيمُ ۞ اَلْخَبِيرُ ۞

اَلْعَلِيُّ ۞ اَلشَّكُورُ ۞ اَلْغَفُورُ ۞

اَلْمُقِيتُ ۞ اَلْحَفِيظُ ۞ اَلْكَبِيرُ ۞

اَلْكَبِيرُ ۞ اَلْجَلِيلُ ۞ اَلْحَسِيبُ ۞

اَلْوَاسِعُ ۞ اَلْمُجِيبُ ۞ اَلرَّقِيبُ ۞

اَلْمَجِيدُ ۞ اَلْوَدُودُ ۞ اَلْحَكِيمُ ۞

CHAPTER 2

MUHAMMAD

ABOU AL-QASIM MUHAMMAD IBN
'ABD ALLAH IBN 'ABD AL-MUTTALIB, THE FULL TITLE
OF MUHAMMAD, THE PROPHET OF ISLAM

THE NAME MUHAMMAD DERIVES FROM THE VERB *HAMADA*, MEANING "TO PRAISE, GLORIFY". MUSLIM HAGIOGRAPHY GIVES him another name, Ahmad.[1] It draws upon a verse of the Qur'an in which Muhammad is heralded by Jesus as a future Prophet. In European languages, other variations are often given: thus, Mahomet is a form of Muhammad, and one also sees Mahommed, Mahound, Mehmet, Mahowne and Machomet.

The Qur'an lists His other attributes. He is the "Warner" of the religion.[2] He is not the Father of any man, but the Messenger of God.[3] It is said of him that he is the "Perfect Model" or the "Perfect Exemplar", as he is called in this verse from sura 33, al-Ahzab, which gives us the fullest portrait of the Prophet Muhammad: "Ye have indeed in the Messenger of Allah a beautiful pattern of conduct for anyone whose hope is in Allah and the Final Day, and who engages much in the praise of Allah" (The Confederates, XXXIII, 21). The Arab oral tradition often calls him the Qurayshi ethnotype, since the Prophet was a member of the powerful pagan tribe of the Quraysh, who ruled Mecca. In this respect, he was the one who put an end to the "Pagan Era" (*'Ahd al-jahilia*), re-established the transcendent "Truth"

of God and, moreover, organised the community of Muslims (*Al-Umma al-islamiyya*, sometimes known as the Muhammadan community); he was their guide, their legislator and their greatest strategist. Muhammad belonged to the clan of Banu Hashîm, which would later be the basis for the family tree of the Hashemites, from which several Arab sovereigns claim to be descended.

Muhammad's date of birth is not certain. It was in the "Year of the Elephant", probably between 569 and 571 A.D. This was a black year, marked by an attack on Mecca led by the Yemeni-Ethiopian general Abraha, a Christian vice-regent, whose army was mounted on elephants.[4] Muhammad was the son of 'Abd Allah and Amina bint Wahb. His father died before his birth, and his mother Amina passed away shortly thereafter, entrusting him to a wet-nurse from the nomadic tribe of Banu Saad, named Halima.[5]

Muhammad was orphaned by the age of five or six and was left poor and destitute, having received no inheritance from his parents. This detail links him, symbolically, with the line of great prophets, all of whom had been poor. He was then taken in by his grandfather, 'Abd al-Muttalib, who was the head of the clan of Banu Hashim at the time, and who looked after him

Preceding double page: Calligraphy of fifty-four of the names of Allah.
Opposite: The arrival of the Prophet in Medina and the building of the mosque. Illustration from a
religious manuscript. Punjab, Lahore, c. 1800. Galerie J. Soustiel.

until his death. Thereafter, the privilege of raising him fell to his paternal uncle, Abu Talib. In fact, since the very strict customs of mutual aid within families were absolutely binding, this was his duty. Muhammad's disrupted childhood is reported thus in the Qur'an: "Did He not find thee an orphan and give thee shelter and care? And He found thee wandering, and gave thee guidance. And He found thee in need, and made thee independent ..." (The Glorious Morning Light, XCIII, 6–8). Soon, however, the Meccans recognised in Muhammad the most pious and accomplished man of his generation and they called him *al-Amin*, "the righteous one" or "the honest one". At the age of twenty, with an unsullied reputation for integrity, Muhammad entered the service of a rich Qurayshi merchant, a woman named Khadija, the daughter of Khawalayd and a distant relative. He drove her caravans to Syria.

By dint of tenacity and probity, he became her right-hand man, managed her affairs and married her in 596. At the time, Muhammad was twenty-five years old, while Khadija was nearly forty. Six children were born from this first marriage, two of them sons who died in infancy. Of the daughters, tradition gives pride of place to Fatima, the favourite, who was the future wife of Ali, the fourth Caliph, and the mother of Hassan and Hussein. Muhammad died in Medina on 8 June 632. Throughout his mission, Muhammad was attacked by the pagan leaders of Mecca, who were members of his own tribe. He was mercilessly persecuted until September 622, the date of his migration to Medina, known as the year 1 A.H.

(After the *Hijra*, [Hegirah] meaning "exile" or "emigration"). In this place of refuge, Yathrib, known thereafter as *Madinat an-Nabi*, Medina ("The City of the Prophet"), he created the first city-state of Islam and its first constitution. It was here, in this city, that the main rituals of Islam evolved.

Two years after the Hijra, the canonical direction of the Kaaba, known as the *qibla*, was fixed. The Prophet's house therefore became the first mosque, while Bilal, a freed black slave, was given the task of calling the Muslims to prayer.

From the eighth century onwards, Muslim hagiographers reported disturbing events which tended to show that a great *baraka* (blessing) illuminated the deeds and actions of Muhammad, long before he perceived the *wahyi*, the supernatural inspiration, divine in nature, which was the basis of the Revelation.

Muslims have a huge body of texts detailing the life and work of the Prophet. They were written exclusively by his close Companions, and later, the best biographers. Called *Sira*, short for the Arabic expression *Sirat al-rasul*, meaning "The Conduct/Life of the Prophet", these apologetics are also the logical basis of the *sunna* (Tradition), which is otherwise known as the consensual "median way" of orthodoxy. What does this mean exactly? This is an important question, since, after the Qur'an, for most Muslims the *sunna* is the principal repository of the law. The *hadith* consist of all the reported speech, thoughts, attitudes or observations made by the Prophet and authenticated as such by a number of first-hand witnesses. Six collections of *hadith*, thought to be "authenticated", were recorded at the end of the eighth century and throughout the ninth century. Two of them, the *Sahih* of Bokhari (810–870) and the *Sahih* of Muslim ibn Hajjaj, are held in higher regard than all the others. Muslims greatly revere scholarly theologians such as Abu Hanifa, the *imam* Ash-Shafi'i, Ibn Hanbal, At-Tirmidhi, Abu Dawud, Ibn Maja, An-Nasa'î, an-Nawani and Malik ibn Anas, who lived between the seventh and thirteenth centuries and have left invaluable writings, such as the famous work by Malik ibn Anas entitled *al-Muwatta.*

As a "Messenger of God" (*Rasul Allah*), Muhammad is, in the eyes of Muslims, the "Seal of the Prophets". He fulfils the monotheistic tradition started by his illustrious predecessors Adam, Abraham, Moses and Jesus: "Muhammad is not the father of any of your men, but he is the Messenger of Allah, and the Seal of the Prophets" (The Confederates, XXXIII, 40).

Muhammad, the founder of Islam, is a universal Prophet and law-giver. His signature is the Qur'an, the revelation with which he was entrusted. His message is fidelity to an unalterable Divine Word; his mission is the establishment of peace on earth.

Yet Muhammad was a warlord and fine strategist, who ended his mission only a few weeks before his death, having fought for more than twenty years against polytheism and his foes. He suffered numerous betrayals and setbacks, converted a large number of pagans and set free dozens of slaves. In Muslim minds, however, the Battle of Badr, from the name of a site in southern Medina, which took place on 17 March 624, tolled the death knell of pagan Arabia because, for the first time, a handful of Muslims defeated the well-trained army of the Quraysh, several hundred strong. On 4 December 656, another memorable battle, the "Battle of the Camel", was fought between 'Ali, the future fourth Caliph, and two enemy high chiefs, supported by 'A'isha. The battle was won by 'Ali.

Muhammad spoke his last words in public on Mount 'Arafat during a farewell pilgrimage, in the very place where, every year, Muslims throng to fulfil one of the five duties of their faith, the *hajj.*

1. "And remember, Jesus, the Son of Mary, said: 'O Children of Israel! I am the Messenger of Allah (sent) to you, confirming the Law (which came) before me, and giving Glad Tidings of a Messenger to come after me, Whose name shall be Ahmad'" (Al-Saff, XLI, 6).
2. "And if any stray, say: 'I am only a Warner'" (The Ants, XXVII, 72).
3. "Muhammad is not the father of any of your men, but (he is) the Messenger of Allah" (The Confederates, XXXIII, 40).
4. "Seest thou not how thy Lord dealt with the Companions of the Elephant?" (The Elephant, CV, 1).
5. This is the traditional genealogy of the Prophet as given by Abu'l-Feda: Abu'l-Qasim Muhammad was the son of Abd al-Muttalib, the son of Hashim, the son of Abd-Menaf, the son of Kossai, the son of Kaleb, the son of Morrah, the son of Ka'b, the son of Luwai, the son of Ghalib, the son of Fakhr or Quraysh, the son of Malik, the son of Nadhr, the son of Kenana, the son of Khuzayma, the son of Mudraka, the son of Ilyâs, the son of Mudhar, the son of Nizar, the son of Ma'd, the son of Adnan, who was the direct descendant of Ishmael, the son of Abraham. Muhammad is also the name of the 47th sura of the Qur'an (XLVII).

CHAPTER 3

THE QUR'AN

THE NON-CREATED AND INCARNATE WORLD
AND DIVINE INSPIRATION

IT WAS IN GHAR HIRA, A CAVE NEAR MECCA, IN THE YEAR 610 OR 611, THAT MUHAMMAD, DURING ONE OF HIS RETREATS, HEARD THE Angel Gabriel, *Jibril* say to him: "Recite, read, announce (*iqrâ*)." Surprised, the Prophet replied: "But I do not know how to read." The Angel Gabriel then asked him to repeat the Word: "Read! In the name of thy Lord and Cherisher, who created—created man, out of a mere clot of congealed blood. Proclaim! And Thy Lord is Most Bountiful—He Who taught (the use of) the Pen—Taught man that which he knew not" (The Blood Clot, XCVI, 1–5).

These then are the first words of this non-created and sublime Word expressed by the Angel Gabriel, announced by the Prophet and transmitted to man by means of reciters (*huffaz*), whose prodigious memories kept it from oblivion.

Revealed in its entirety in the "perspicuous"[1] Arabic tongue, the language of Hijaz, and not allowing a single alteration, addition or deletion, the Qur'an is the Book *par excellence*, the Book about which no doubt can be permitted (the *rayba fihi*), because doubts in this area amount to lack of faith. "This is the Book; in it is guidance sure, without doubt, to those who fear Allah. [...] And as to those who reject Faith, it is the same to them

whether thou warn them or do not warn them; they will not believe. Allah hath set a seal on their hearts and on their hearing, and on their eyes is a veil; Great is the penalty they (incur)" (The Cow, II, 1–6).

Moreover, the *mushaf*, the physical Qur'an which we can consult and touch is, in the eyes of Muslim esotericists, only the visible copy, the divine archetype, of that *materia prima* which has been safeguarded for all eternity in a Preserved Tablet.[2] The word *Qu'rân* comes from the verb *qaraa* and the noun *qirâ'a*, meaning reading or recitation, recalling the dictation of the text by the Archangel to the Prophet which began around 610–611 and ended in 632 A.D.

The Qur'an was revealed successively, first in Mecca—this revelation is called the "first period" (611–622)—and then at Medina, in what is known as the "second period" (622–632). It consists of one hundred and fourteen chapters, called *suras*, and six thousand two hundred and nineteen verses, the *ayat*. The basic element of the Qur'an, the verse, is a powerful sign which is an assurance of the divine presence. It is derived etymologically from "miracle" and signifies the realisation of an infinitely superior will. Within the Qur'an, the suras are grouped together into sixty distinct

The Qur'an, a large manuscript in the Arabic naskhi script, with insertions in the Persian nastaliq script. Iran, c. 1820. Galerie J. Soustiel.

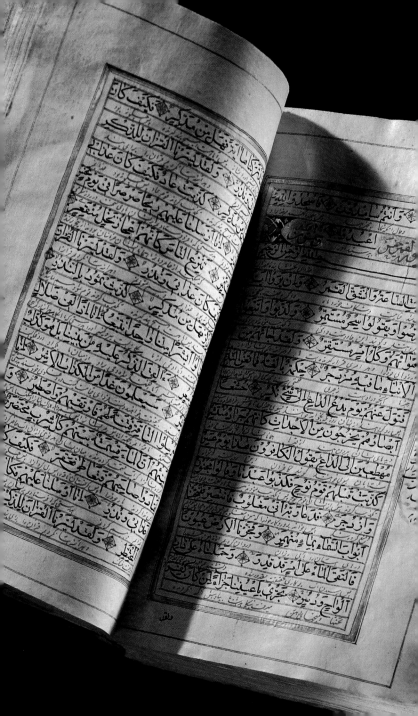

بِسْمِ اللهِ الرَّحْمٰنِ الرَّحِيمِ

الٓمٓ ۚ ذٰلِكَ الْكِتَابُ لَا رَيْبَ ۛ فِيهِ ۛ هُدًى
لِّلْمُتَّقِينَ ۝ الَّذِينَ يُؤْمِنُونَ بِالْغَيْبِ
وَيُقِيمُونَ الصَّلَاةَ وَمِمَّا رَزَقْنَاهُمْ يُنفِقُونَ ۝
وَالَّذِينَ يُؤْمِنُونَ بِمَا أُنزِلَ إِلَيْكَ وَمَا
أُنزِلَ مِن قَبْلِكَ وَبِالْآخِرَةِ هُمْ يُوقِنُونَ ۝
أُولٰئِكَ عَلَىٰ هُدًى مِّن رَّبِّهِمْ ۖ وَأُولٰئِكَ هُمُ الْمُفْلِحُونَ ۝

بِسْمِ اللهِ الرَّحْمَنِ الرَّحِيمِ

اَلْحَمْدُ لِلهِ رَبِّ الْعَالَمِينَ ۞ الرَّحْمَنِ الرَّحِيمِ ۞

مَالِكِ يَوْمِ الدِّينِ ۞ إِيَّاكَ نَعْبُدُ

وَإِيَّاكَ نَسْتَعِينُ ۞ اهْدِنَا الصِّرَاطَ

الْمُسْتَقِيمَ ۞ صِرَاطَ الَّذِينَ

أَنْعَمْتَ عَلَيْهِمْ ۞ غَيْرِ الْمَغْضُوبِ

عَلَيْهِمْ وَلَا الضَّالِّينَ ۞

sections of varying lengths called *ahzab.* The longest, from the second sura (The Cow) to the seventy-first (Noah), may contain up to several hundred verses. The longest sura in the Qur'an is that of the Cow, which is two hundred and eighty-six verses long. The medium-sized chapters are those from sura LXXX (He Frowned) to sura XCII (The Night). Some of the shortest chapters consist of only three verses. They range from sura XCIII (The Glorious Morning Light) to sura CXIV (Mankind), the last sura of the Holy Book, which has six verses. Each section, except the ninth,[3] begins with an invocation to Allah, the *basmala*, the symbolic key which slots into the Qur'anic mystery. The inauguration of the whole, the *fatiha* (which means "The Opening", or "The Introduction") is one of the most frequently recited suras. Its seven verses (see page 9) bear the prestigious title of "Mother of the Book", since, according to a tradition of the Prophet, it is a distillation of its richness and complexity.

The Prophet's scribe, Zayd ibn Thabit, is believed to have recorded the basis for what later evolved into the vulgate of the Qur'an by order of the Caliph 'Uthman, between 644 and 656.

Since then, the Qur'an has been sung and chanted in the mosques, as well as copied, meditated upon, interpreted and learned by heart in the Qur'anic schools (*madâris*). It has also been very widely translated.[4] Learning the Qur'an by heart is a greatly blessed act for all Muslims. It is often a prerequisite for Qur'anic exegesis, and for Islamic theology and jurisprudence. This powerful text, which takes the form of a continuous

stream of consciousness and an uninterrupted explanation, this "great miracle", has at its heart an irrefutable aesthetic argument: "And if ye are in doubt as to what We have revealed from time to time to Our servant, then produce a surah like thereunto; and call your witnesses or helpers (if there are any) besides Allah, if your (doubts) are true" (The Cow, II, 23).

1. "The tongue of him they wickedly point to is notably foreign, while this is Arabic, pure and clear" (Bees, XVI, 103).
2. "Nay, this is a Glorious Qu'ran (inscribed) in a Tablet Preserved!" (The Constellations, CXXXV, 22).
3. The sura entitled "The Repentance" or "The Disavowal".
4. Since its translation into Latin in the Middle Ages, the Qur'an has gradually been translated into all the languages known to man. However, the greatest number of translations, and the most accurate, date from the end of the last century and from the present century. Apart from French, which counts no fewer than twelve important translations, German and English, the following should also be noted: Finnish (1942), Afrikaans (1950), Basque (1952), Gallic, Lowland Scottish (1948) and Yiddish, in Hebrew script (1950). There have also been versions in Platt Deutsch (1698), Swiss Romansch (1949), and Volapuk (the universal language invented in 1879 by Johann Martin Schleyer) in 1951. Translations also exist, among others, in Hindi, Uzbek, Chinese, Malinké, Swahili and Peuhl.

Preceding double page: The Qur'an, a small manuscript in the Arabic naskhi script. Frontispiece showing the fatiha and the opening of the second sura, Turkey, Ottoman Art, early eighteenth century. Galerie J. Soustiel. Opposite: The Qur'an in the Paris Mosque.

إذا الله عن

لا الا الله

CHAPTER 4

THE PROFESSION OF FAITH

THE CORNERSTONE OF ALL BELIEF IN ISLAM, THE *SHAHADA* IS ALSO THE STARTING POINT OF ISLAMIC DOGMA

THE *SHAHADA*, A REAL JEWEL OF FAITH, IS IN A SPIRITUAL SENSE MUHAMMAD'S MOST IMPORTANT CONTRIBUTION. IT CONSISTS OF SAYING the following phrase: "There is no god but God and Muhammad is the Messenger of God".

Shahada means "to affirm", "to attest", but also "to bear witness to the existence and unity of God". It is the Muslim's most intimate act of piety, the manifest sign of his adherence to the faith of the one true God, the means whereby the faith of the individual is grafted onto the branch of communal faith and the believer is released from his selfish instincts and the narcissism which assails him.[1]

It requires a precondition which Muslims call "the good (or praiseworthy) intention" (*niyya*). A saying of the Prophet brings this home with full force: "No act is valid without good intention and each being will be judged according to this intention."[2]

The very edifice of faith is built on this *niyya*, the primal intention which can be defined by an expression imbued with psychology: "sincere frame of mind" or *sidq*. The *niyya*, like the *shahada* which crowns it, obviously excludes all ostentation or blameworthy action. Even today, any adult who is sound of mind and pronounces this formula with conviction becomes a Muslim in the eyes of Divine Law, since "The only Believers are those who have believed in Allah and his Messenger, and have never since doubted" (The Chambers, XLIX, 15).

While the *shahada* is the simplest act of the Muslim faith, it is also the most important. It influences the dogma on which the religion is built, since it is understood that faith begins with the recitation of this phrase. It is notably the manifestation of the divine attributes since everything about the Creator is brought back to life by the love that the believers give Him. It is reported that, according to Abu Sa'îd El-Khodri, a Muslim came to see the Prophet and asked him if it were enough to recite the phrase in the Qur'an: "Say: he is Allah, the One and Only" (The Purity of Faith, CXII, 1). Understanding that the believer was afraid of not fulfilling the conditions of the dogma, the Prophet Muhammad is said to have answered: "By the One who holds my soul in His hands, these few words are equal to one third of the Qur'an."[3]

Thus the act of testifying both to the unity of God (the first *shahada*) and to the authenticity of the Prophetic message (the second *shahada*) are acts which, on the one hand, imply the deep awareness of the believer, and, on the other, his

Muslim prayer calls for a set of characteristic gestures, each with its own meaning.

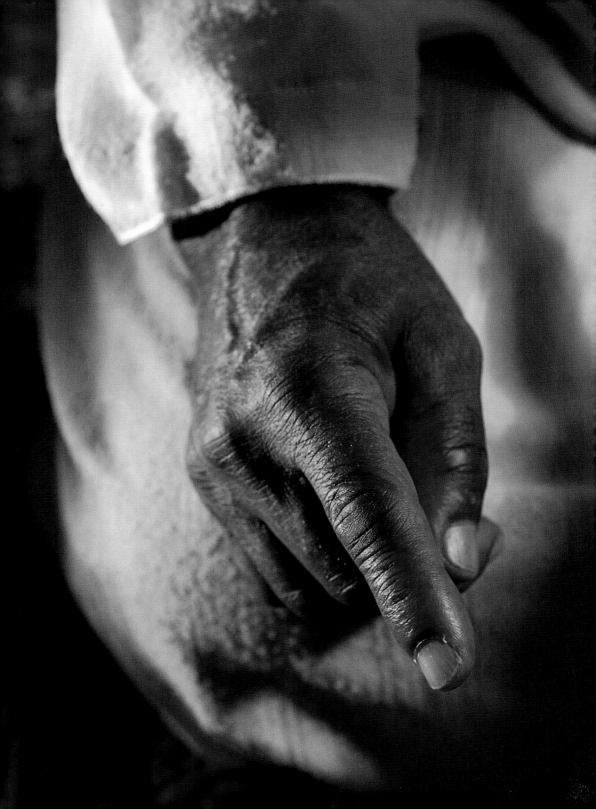

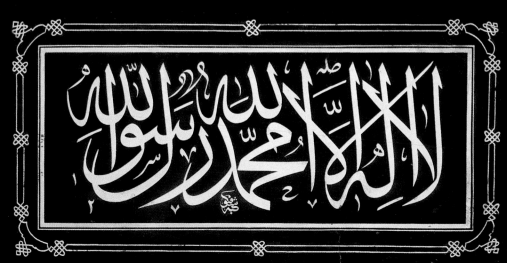

responsibility. These professions are absolutely meaningless if they are gained by constraint, mental manipulation or any other subterfuge: "O ye who believe! Believe in Allah and His Messenger, and the scripture which He hath sent to His Messenger and the scripture which He sent to those before (him). Any who denieth Allah, His angels, His Books, His Messengers, and the Day of Judgement, hath gone far, far astray" (The Women, IV, 136).

As well as being a blessed phrase, the *shahada* is also one of the means, surely the most certain, of gaining ever more sincerity in the exercise of the religion. One passes from the simple formula which consists in saying with conviction the names of Allah and of the Prophet, to the very content of this pronouncement, to its spiritual significance. For Muslims, each human act can lead the faithful either to good or to evil. Faith alone is essential to keep him in the blessing of Allah.

This faith is manifold. Fulfilling the conditions of faith takes different forms: not being slanderous, a liar or envious is an act of faith; seeking peace and harmony, preaching justice among men and showing tolerance for others are acts of faith. Sincerely wishing the presence of one's fellow man, succouring the weak and giving alms are also acts of faith. One *hadith* in fact tells us that "faith consists of sixty and some branches".[4]

Fundamentally, the profession of faith is the synthesis of the whole life of the individual. At the same time, as it symbolises his conviction at a given moment, it makes him an active member of the congregation of believers. This explains why the *shahada* is both the first condition of Islam and the formula which the believer must say when he feels that his time has come, on his deathbed. It is the key to earthly life yet it is also the phrase which offers passage to the world to come.

An authorised tradition claims that this phrase is the repetition of the first phrase spoken by the Angel Gabriel and learnt by the Prophet.

1. The points which the Qur'an has in common with Christianity and Judaism are: the same God, the same intercessory Angel, Gabriel (Jibril), Adam and Eve (Hawa). Islam has a sincere respect for the prophets who came before Muhammad, some of whom are referred to by name in the Qur'an: Abraham (Ibrahim), the Ancestor, father of Ishmael (Isma'il) and Isaac (Ishaq), Jesus ('Isa), David (Dawud) and Joseph (Yusuf), and for Mary (Maryam). Others are merely evoked: Elijah, John, Job, Jonas, Saul, Zachariah ... Islam recognizes the authenticity of the holy books, especially the Bible and the Qur'an. On the other hand, the trinity Father, Son and Holy Ghost is denied, since Allah, the One God, cannot be multiplied nor have progeny. For Moslems this would be like anthropomorphism, and a heresy.
2. *Hadith* of the Prophet.
3. *Ibid.*
4. *Ibid.*

Calligraphy of the shahada.
Above, work of Sayyid Muhammad Hasan, 1897–98. Below, work of Shekif in 1860–61.
Turkey. The Nasser D. Khalili Collection of Islamic Art.

CHAPTER 5

PRAYER

TO PRAY IS TO ACCEPT ISLAM AS THE RELIGION OF THE ONE GOD AND MUHAMMAD HIS PROPHET

PRAYER IS ONE OF THE FIVE PILLARS OF ISLAM, IMMEDIATELY FOLLOWING THE PROFESSION OF FAITH. PRAYER IS PERFORMED FIVE TIMES a day, and it represents the most visible form of the believer's attachment to his faith.

In principle, collective prayer is more meritorious than individual prayer, the former, it is said, having twenty-seven times the spiritual value of the latter. From this, therefore, ensues the importance of the Friday prayer, *al-Jumu'a*, the day of the (great) gathering of the community.

The Qur'an states that this rite can only be performed when physical and spiritual safety are assured: "When ye are free from danger, set up Regular Prayers: For such prayers are enjoined on Believers at stated times" (The Women, IV, 103).

The daily cycle begins at sunset and ends at the same time on the following day. The times of daily prayers thus correspond to the rising, zenith and setting of the sun. There are five ritual prayers:
- As-Subh, performed between dawn and sunrise
- Az-Zuhr, performed when the sun is at its zenith
- Al-'Asr, performed in the afternoon
- Al-Maghrib, performed at sundown
- Al-'Isha', performed during the evening, before going to bed.

When praying, the two sexes are kept in perfect decency. If prayer is being performed at home, the prayer-carpet and surroundings must be spotlessly clean. Indeed, Muslim prayer is only valid when the believer is surrounded by the precise conditions of purification, which calls for a series of ablutions: "O ye who believe! When ye prepare for prayer, wash your faces, and your hands (and arms) to the elbows; and (wash) your feet to the ankles" (The Repast, V, 6).

The current ritual of ablution is carried out in a precise order. The believer must consciously decide to perform the ablutions with a view to prayer. He must then say the *basmala*, "In the name of Allah", the formula of devotion to God. Only then can the actual ablutions begin. These involve the hands, mouth, nose, face, ears, forearms, head and feet.

Each action is repeated three times, beginning with the right-hand side, which is sacred throughout the eastern and Semitic tradition. This ceremonial washing clearly shows that water enjoys a symbolic status which far outstrips its merely hygienic function. There is also a "dry ablution", purification with earth or sand. When the Muslim finds himself without water, he is permitted to use a pebble or a fistful of sand: "If ye are in a state of

"And Allah has made the earth for you as a carpet (spread out)"
(Noah, LXXI, 19).

ceremonial impurity [...] and ye find no water, then take for yourselves clean sand or earth, and rub therewith your faces and hands" (The Repast, V, 6).

However, ritual purity has its reverse side. It is breached each time the believer becomes sullied, wittingly or unwittingly. In certain cases—sexual intercourse, childbirth or menstruation—the believer is called upon to wash completely, according to a practice called *ghusl*, which is as codified as the ritual of ablutions.

But prayer is an act of faith every time it is observed, not only according to the canonical dictates of purification, time and place, but particularly when it arises from the ardent desire of the believer. Each prayer comprises several cycles (*raq'a*, pl. *riqa'*), which follow each other in the same order:
– initial upright position, hands raised to the level of the face
– bowing forwards from the waist, with the hands resting on the knees
– double prostration, with the hands on the prayer-mat
– return to the upright position.

After two, three or four *riqa'*, the prayer ends with a *jalsâ* or seated position. Thus, once the believer has placed himself in the protection of God and reaffirmed His power by a formula known as *takbir* ("Allah is Most Great"), he continues his worship with the recital of the *fatiha*, the opening sura of the Qur'an, and of another sura, long or short, depending upon the occasion. Finally, there are several phrases of blessing and grace. The glorification of God (*tasbih*) is short: "Glory be to our Lord the Most High", as is the

formula of thanksgiving: "Allah hears him who thanks Him, our Lord, praise be to You." There then follows the *shahada* and the *taslim*, which is a final salutation.

Other than these five daily prayers, a limited number of additional prayers are recommended.

The call to prayer (*adhan*) is also made five times a day. Inaugurated during the lifetime of the Prophet himself, this call was first made by a freed Abyssinian slave named Bilal. He is thus the first *muezzin* (*mu'adhdhin*) in Muslim history.

Within the context of canonical prayer, which the Prophet is said to have preferred to all the goods of this world, the part played by meditation, whether individual (*du'a*) or collective (*zikr*), is important to note.

Collective prayer performed outside the mosque in the El-Hussein Square, Cairo, Egypt, 1994.

CHAPTER 6

ALMSGIVING

THE ISLAMIC THEORY AND PRACTICE OF GIVING

LAWFUL ALMSGIVING, WHICH IS THE IMPLE-
MENTATION OF SHARING GOODS ACQUIRED
IN THIS WORLD AND CONSIDERED AS DIVINE
bounties, is one of the perfections demanded by
Islam, and one of its five conditions of validity.

There are two categories of alms. The first,
zakat, is compulsory.[1] It is mentioned in the Qur'an:
"Of their goods take alms, that so thou mightest
purify and sanctify them" (The Repast, IX, 103),
and is the most succinct expression of the link
between almsgiving and purification. It is calcu-
lated on the basis of actual possessions, property,
capital and income which are subject to donation
and sharing.

This is an annual almsgiving, legal, codified
and imposed upon every adult Muslim, regardless
of sex or origin. This first category of alms is thus
equivalent to a tax on all Muslims to be donated
to the community and to the public Treasury as an
expression of solidarity between the different
social classes.

The Qur'an specifies: "Alms are for the poor
and needy, and those employed to administer the
funds; for those whose hearts have recently been
reconciled (to the Truth); for those in bondage
and in debt; in the cause of Allah; and for the
wayfarer" (The Repentance, IX, 60). Alms have

evolved with society and been adapted to the his-
toric and economic conditions prevailing under
Islam. Nowadays, there are no captives to be
bought out of bondage or wayfarers to rescue. On
the other hand, a new poverty, especially in the
cities, has become very apparent. Today, spending
goes on the disadvantaged social classes. The best
alms are not those which "cost" the most materi-
ally, but those given with the greatest fervour and
conviction.

In the early days of Islam, a small group of very
poor Muslims came to see the Prophet to discuss
the case of rich dignitaries who not only scrupulously observed their Islamic duties but also
devoted a proportion of their goods to substantial
almsgiving. The Prophet answered them in these
terms: "Has not Allah given you the means
wherewith to give alms? In truth, each *tasbih* is an
almsgiving, each *takbir* is an almsgiving, each *tahmid* is an almsgiving, each *tahlil* is an almsgiving.
Commanding good is an almsgiving. And in the
work of the flesh of each one of you there is an
almsgiving."[2] *Tasbih, takbir, tahmid* and *tahlil* are
the current forms of praisegiving which are part of
Muslim prayer and which, in this regard, are regu-
larly recited by the faithful. Some renowned
theologians such as El-Bokhari (810–870), Razi

Spontaneous almsgiving (sadaqa) *independent of the annual tax* (zakat).

(1149–1209), Qortubi (d. 1273), etc., consider that *zakat* has the power to multiply the goods of those who give it with sincerity.

The Holy Book also reminds us that one can "atone for" one's sins by means of the annual donation, for this has the same value as repentance: "But (even so), if they repent, establish regular prayers and practise regular charity—they are your brethren in Faith" (The Repentance, IX, 11).

Finally, a Prophetic tradition reported by El-Bokhari shows the importance of *zakat* in the popular representations of the next world: "He to whom God has given goods and who has not paid his tithe, God will, on the Day of Resurrection, make his goods appear in the form of a python with a bald head and two excrescences of flesh. On the Day of Resurrection, this python will coil itself around the neck of that man; it will seize him in its jaws and say: 'I am your goods, I am your treasure'."[3]

The second category of almsgiving, the *sadaqa*, is a spontaneous donation which can be made just as well to a beggar who holds out his hand in a *souk* as to a needy branch of the family. Here too, in order to be considered a pious act, the *sadaqa* must be made with legitimate funds and honest gain. It must be given without ostentation, so discreetly, indeed, that the left hand must be totally unaware of the donation being made with the right hand. In addition, the Qur'an specifies that "By no means shall ye attain righteousness unless ye give (freely) of that which ye love; and whatever ye give, of a truth Allah knoweth it well" (The Family of 'Imran, III, 92).

These two forms of alsmgiving are associated with prayer, and of equal value to it, and just as meritorious in the eyes of God as testified by the Prophet. They are evoked in over eighty verses of the Qur'an in thirty-four suras, an abundance of references which clearly demonstrates the centrality of almsgiving in Muslim dogma.

1. Most probable etymology: "To purify oneself", from the root z-k-a, *zakka* or *tazakka* meaning both "to fulfil one's alms" and "to purify oneself", in conformity with the Qur'anic text that says: "But those will prosper who purify themselves, and glorify the name of their Guardian-Lord, and lift their hearts in prayer" (The Most High, LXXXVII, 14–15).

2. *Hadith* of the Prophet.

3. El-Bokhari, vol. 1, p. 455.

The person giving alms should not know how much his hand is donating.

CHAPTER 7

THE FAST

ABSTINENCE FROM FOOD AND DRINK IN ORDER
TO BE IN HARMONY WITH THE SPIRIT OF ISLAM AND TO SHARE
THE DISTRESS OF THE MOST UNDERPRIVILEGED

THE FAST OF RAMADAN, THE NINTH MONTH OF THE MUSLIM CALENDAR, IS DESIGNED AS DEPRIVATION FROM FOOD, BUT IT IS A desired and accepted deprivation. This is the holy month during which the Qur'an was revealed: "Ramadan is the (month) in which was sent down the Qu'ran, as a guide to mankind, also clear (Signs) for guidance and judgement (between right and wrong)" (The Cow, II, 185).

According to ancient custom, the word *ramadan* has also come to mean the practice of fasting itself, and as such often, and incorrectly, replaces the word *sawm*, which means "abstinence": "O ye who believe! Fasting is prescribed to you as it was prescribed to those before you, that ye may (learn) self-restraint" (The Cow, II, 183).

The month of Ramadan, which is the fourth Pillar of Islam, is obligatory for all believers, male or female, from puberty onwards. The sick, nursing mothers, pregnant women and travellers are all exempt, nor are mentally ill and young children bound by the fast. On the other hand, those who only have a temporary reason for being unable to fast, such as menstruating women, or anyone who cannot fast for other reasons such as medical treatment, must make up the days of fasting they have missed in the course of the year.

The start of the lawful fast is established as soon as a worthy believer sees the form of the crescent moon. In fact, it has been decreed that: "Every one of you who is present (at his home) during that month should spend it in fasting" (The Cow, II, 185).

The crescent moon, the ancient emblem of the Sassanids, has gradually become the special symbol of Islam. Although it had for long figured in the coats of arms of the Ottoman Empire, it became associated with the emblems of other Muslim countries only in the nineteenth century. The tradition has persisted, but since the science of astronomy has allowed Arabs to calculate the appearance of the moon with a certain reliability (the first observatory was built in Baghdad in 820), the contribution of scientists has been accepted. However, each time that there is recourse to the letter of the Qur'an, actually observing the new moon highly motivates the faithful, as it augurs a month of beneficial fasting. Nowadays, this practice is naturally more widespread in desert regions and in the countryside than in the cities.

The actual fast begins a little before dawn (*fajr*) and ends after sundown (*imsak*), at the time of the first evening prayer (*maghrib*). The faithful

The crescent moon (hilal) announces the holy month of Ramadan, but astronomical calculations and the unanimous opinion of scientists tends to be more and more the point of reference.

may take a light meal before daybreak. Widely-used manuals give the starting and ending times of the fast. Nowadays, they are also broadcast on radio or television, especially in the cities, in Muslim countries, as well as for Muslims living in non-Muslim countries.

During the hours of fasting, before the break-ing of the fast (*iftar*) is announced, the Muslim abstains from eating, smoking and drinking. He is also prohibited from having sexual intercourse, even within a legitimate union. The same is true of a whole series of antisocial behaviour con-demned by common morality (for example, back-biting, envy, stealing, quarrelling, rivalry or lying). Committing these acts annuls the spiritual value of the fast.

The twenty-seventh night of Ramadan, the Night of Power (*Laylat al-Qadr*), is very impor-tant, since it is the night on which Revelation was first made: "We have indeed revealed this (Mes-sage) in the Night of Power. And what will explain to thee what the Night of Power is? The Night of Power is better than a thousand months. Therein come down the angels and the Spirit by Allah's permission, on every errand: Peace! ... This until the rise of Morn" (The Night of Power, XCVII).

Ramadan is also the month of grace, of great religious fervour and a time for forgiveness. Col-lective mutual aid is given more overtly and more frequently. The most devout observers of the fast go to the mosque and spend part of the night in a supplementary prayer called *Salat al-Tawarih* or the Prayer of Relaxation or Rest.

Despite the demands the month of ritual fast-ing makes, Muslims approach it with joy, trust and serenity. According to Abu-Horayra (seventh century), the Prophet said: "When Ramadan begins, the gates of heaven open, the gates of hell are closed and the demons are chained up."[1]

1. El-Bokhari, vol. 1, p. 607.

Ritual foods are meticulously codified in Islam.
Dried fruits and sweets are not prohibited.

CHAPTER 8

THE PILGRIMAGE

MEETING THE COMMUNITY OF BELIEVERS
IN THE HOUSE OF GOD

AFTER THE PROFESSION OF FAITH, PRAYER, ALMSGIVING AND THE FAST, PILGRIMAGE TO MECCA IS THE FIFTH AND LAST PILLAR OF ISLAM. It is enjoined upon all adult Muslims of either sex, who have the material means to undertake it, even if only once in their lives.[1]

The great pilgrimage (al-Hajj) consists of several stages spread out over a number of days, usually from the eighth to the twelfth day of Dhu'l-Hijja, the twelfth month of the Muslim calendar. The period mentioned in the Qur'an is a sacral period, that is, subject to minutely codified purification rituals, the most apparent being those which concern dress and costume. The following saying of the Prophet is reported by 'Abdallah ben 'Omar (seventh century): "The man in the state of ihram must put on neither qamis, nor turban, nor trousers, nor burnous, nor any clothing which has been touched by saffron or by the ouers (a plant dye), nor boots, unless he cannot find any shoes; in which case, he must cut his boots down to below his ankles."[2]

The Muslim pilgrimage consists of five stages. The strict observance of this route is the only guarantee of the validity of the pilgrimage:

I. DEPARTURE FOR 'ARAFAT (8 Dhu'l-Hijja), the holy mountain of Islam situated 13 miles from Mecca. Upon arrival in Mecca, the believer must cleanse himself (ihram) by removing his usual clothing and dressing in white robes made of unsewn material and by observing the major prohibitions of spilt blood, sexual intercourse and the practice of hunting. In addition: "Let there be no obscenity, nor wickedness, nor wrangling in the Hajj ..." (The Cow, II, 197).

The pilgrim circumambulates the Kaaba seven times on foot (tawaf). These circumambulations may be undertaken in the company of a professional guide (mutawif). He then prays to God using prayers and invocations, of which the best known and most important is the talbiyya.[3] This cycle is completed with a prayer at the Station of Abraham, which is on the esplanade of the Kaaba.

Finally, the pilgrim must undertake a sevenfold "running" (sa'y) between Safa and Marwa, two small hillocks which are part of the rite. This passage to and fro recalls that of Hagar when, in a panic, she had to find water for her son Ishmael. To keep him from certain death, Allah made a spring of fresh water gush up in front of her near

Crowd of pilgrims on their way to Mecca.

the *mataf*, the path around the Kaaba, where a large portico, recalling the "race" run by Hagar, marks the entrance today. Full of *baraka*, this briny water is called Zamzam. The pilgrims take some home with them in little jars known as *zamzamiyat*.

II. STANDING ON 'ARAFAT (9 *Dhu'l-Hijja*). The pilgrims gather in 'Arafat around the hill of al-Rahma and pray to God throughout the day, particularly reciting the *talbiyya*. This standing on the ninth day of *Dhu'l-Hijja* is important. It recalls the last public act of the Prophet when, during his "Pilgrimage of Farewell", he went up Mount 'Arafat to make his final speech and deliver this Revelation: "This day have I perfected your Religion for you, completed my favour upon you, and have chosen for you Islam as your religion" (The Repast, V, 3). After the afternoon prayers, the pilgrims stand and invoke divine compassion, because, according to tradition, standing on 'Arafat is the culmination of the pilgrimage. It must not be missed on any pretext. After sunset, the pilgrims leave 'Arafat and head for Mina, three and a half miles from Mecca. At the halfway point of their journey, the pilgrims stop at Muzdalifa, where they spend the night. This is an impressive journey for the pilgrims, especially for the more elderly who often require help from a third party. Indeed, the *nafr* is more than a dispersal or a walk, it is a real stampede, the significance of which goes back to the rhythm adopted by the Prophet himself, who accelerated or slowed his pace according to the stages of the ritual.

III. THE DAY OF THE SACRIFICE (*Yawm al-nahr*), MUZDALIFA (10 *Dhu'l-Hijja*). This is the ritual of the immolation of the animal sacrifice which is observed on the same day throughout the Muslim world. This sacrifice is in homage to the act of Abraham who, tested by God, almost sacrificed his eldest son Ishmael. Indeed, contrary to the story told in Genesis,[4] it was Ishmael and not Isaac who, Muslims believe, was the subject of the Archangel's barter during Abraham's sacrifice.[5] God, in His great leniency, having despatched the Angel Gabriel, substituted a sheep for the beloved child, which has been used ever since in this ritual. This, at least, is what most traditional commentators of the Qur'an maintain. Ishmael is considered to be the ancestor of the Bedouin Arabs and the father of their nation. Moreover, an ancestral tradition holds that Ishmael helped his father when he saw that the Holy Temple of the Kaaba was crumbling and falling into ruin and so rebuilt it.

IV. JOURNEY TO MINA (11 *Dhu'l-Hijja*). This is where the day of meditation (*tarwiya*) takes place, and sometimes continues through the following two days (twelfth and thirteenth days of *Dhu'l-Hijja*). An ancestral and obligatory rite accompanies this stage. This is the stoning of Satan (*rajm al-shaytân*) with stones gathered the previous day in Muzdalifa. The devil is symbolised by three upright slabs, the largest of which is permanently covered with a heap of small pebbles. After painstakingly observing this whole journey, the pilgrim deconsecrates himself, sacrificing all or part of his hair

Pilgrim dressed in the white robe of ihram on the hill of al-Rahma on Mount 'Arafat.

(many shave their heads completely), and thus ridding himself of all the taboos which still bind him. These routes and rituals, which are so heavily annotated, have a particular meaning. The circumambulation of the Holy House represents the circumambulation of the angels around the heavenly throne, since, according to Ghazali, "the House of God is a visible symbol in the world of the Kingdom of God which is hidden from sight."[6] Qur'anic exegesis examines all the stages of the pilgrimage in this way, seeing in each a multi-layered significance: manifest, secret, deep, very deep... Only some of the initiated can understand, or, even more, interpret this last degree.

Apart from the great pilgrimage, Muslims also undertake the 'umra, the so-called "small" or "minor pilgrimage", because it is performed only in the Haram, in Mecca and its immediate surroundings. Both these pilgrimages are mentioned in the Qur'an, which distinguishes them from a mere visit to the holy places (ziyara): "Complete the Hajj or Umrah in the service of Allah. But if ye are prevented therefrom, send an offering for sacrifice, such as ye may find, and do not shave your heads until the offering reaches the place of sacrifice. And if any of you is ill, or has an ailment in his scalp (necessitating shaving), he should compensate therefor either by fasting, or by feeding the poor, or by offering a sacrifice" (The Cow, II, 196).

While it is important for pious Muslims, the 'umra is left to the discretion of every individual. It can be undertaken at any time during the liturgical year, except during the period of the Hajj, although preference is given to the seventh month (Rajab),

which is one of the four "holy months."[7] Although this is an act of great blessedness, accruing great advantage to whoever undertakes it, the 'umra is not a substitute for the hajj, which can alone confer the title and prestige of the perfect Muslim.

The spiritual strength of the pilgrimage stems from its total immersion of the pilgrim in the sacred sanctuary. It is also the opportunity for pilgrims to encounter the huge Muslim community, al-umma al-islamiyya, men and women, millions of whom converge from all over the world—who honour the same God.

1. "Pilgrimage [...] is a duty men owe to Allah—those who can afford the journey" (The Family of 'Imran, III, 97).
2. El-Bokhari, vol. 4, p. 99.
3. "Here am I near to you, O my God, here am I" (labayna alla-huma labbayk).
4. Genesis (34: 1–14).
5. Those ranged in ranks, XXXVII, 100–113.
6. M. Hamidullah, "Le pèlerinage à La Mecque", in Les Pèlerinages. (Paris, Seuil: 1950).
7. Mentioned in the Qur'an (The Repentance, IX, 36), these months are: Muharram, the first month, Rajab, the seventh month, Dhu'l-Qa'da, the eleventh month, and Dhu'l-Hijja, the twelfth month. Also called the months of "God's Truce", they carried a number of prohibitions in ancient Arabian times, amongst them inter-tribal warfare.

Léon Adolphe Auguste Belly, Pilgrims to Mecca, 1861. Musée d'Orsay Collection.

CHAPTER 9

MECCA

BIRTHPLACE OF THE PROPHET,
THE PLACE OF DIVINE REVELATION AND THE SITE
OF THE HOLY PILGRIMAGE

FOR EVERY MUSLIM, MECCA—FORMERLY KNOWN AS BAKKAH—A CITY IN THE HEART OF THE MINERAL PLATEAU OF HIJAZ, AT 21°26'17" latitude and 37°54'45" longitude, symbolises the vibrant centre of Islam.

In the Qur'an it is written: "The first house (of worship) appointed for men was that at Bakkah; full of blessing and of guidance for all kinds of beings. In it are signs manifest; (for example), the Station of Abraham; whoever enters it attains security; pilgrimage thereto is a duty men owe to Allah—those who can afford the journey" (The Family of 'Imran, III, 96–97).

The erstwhile name of the town was "Mother of Cities" or "Metropolis of the World" (*Umm al-qurâ'*), which is equivalent to the Greek Ompha-los, but it was also called "The Navel of the World", particularly by Arab geographers of the Middle Ages. Muslims call it by the prestigious name of "Noble Mecca" (*Makka al-muqarrama*), a reference to the four great events that took place there: the birth of the Prophet, the Qur'anic Revelation, the establishment of the *qibla*, and the annual pilgrimage.

The history of Mecca is a very ancient one, particularly in trading and literary terms, which prepared it for the part it would play at the incep-tion of Islam in the seventh century A.D. It is sometimes known by honorific names such as *al-Bayt al-'Atîq* (the Ancient Place), *al-Balad al-Amin* (the Sure Country), *al-Bayt al-Harâm* (the Forbidden City/The Sacred House), or simply *al-Haram* (The Forbidden City), *al-Muqadassa* (the Holiest of Cities), and so on.

It was here that the Prophet was born and lived until he was chosen by God, when he was about forty years of age. The quintessence of the divine, Mecca is considered in theological terms the cradle of the first Qur'anic Revelation, the second having been imparted in Medina. This explains the divi-sion of the Qur'an into Meccan and Medinan suras, the place of revelation being systematically indicated at the start of each chapter, along with the number of verses it contains. Although Mecca is geographically situated in an extremely arid desert region, it is nonetheless the centre of gravity for several holy places such as Safa, Marwa, the cave of Hira, Muzdalifa, the Hill of Light and, fur-ther away, Mount 'Arafat. All these places are extremely important for pilgrimage.

Mecca, where the first conversions to the Muhammadan religion were performed, witnessed its victories and defeats, its great rallying cries and rivalries. It is also the city which persecuted the

Overleaf and opposite: Every year, Mecca welcomes millions of pilgrims scrupulously following the stages which will confer upon them the prestigious title of "hajji".

first Muslims and eventually drove them out to Medina. Later, it would be reinstated by the Prophet, who consecrated it definitively as the centre of the Islamic universe. Mecca was also the epicentre of a whole network of holy cities which have been concentrically scattered throughout the Muslim Empire since its expansion between the eighth and twelfth centuries.

Among them, in order of importance, are Mecca, Medina,[1] called in ancient times Yathrîb— also known as the "Resplendent" (al-Munawara)— and Jerusalem (al-Quds), the three chief holy cities of Islam. Medina, which contains the tomb of the Prophet, was the first city state of Islam, as the community of Muhammad was established there in 623. To this first holy trinity a second circle of holy cities, most of them Shi'ite, can be added:

– Qum, in Iran, where the sixteenth-century tomb of Fatima, the sister of the eighth Shi'i *imam*, is situated;
– Karbala', Iraq, about 60 miles south-west of Baghdad, the place of the martyrdom of Hussein, the son of 'Ali, killed in 680, in an infamous battle;
– Najaf, Iraq, near Kufa on the outskirts of Karbala', the site of the tomb of 'Ali (600–661), the fourth Caliph of Islam and son-in-law of the Prophet.

Finally, over a wider geographic range, there are cities or capitals which have played an important part in the propagation of Islam. The most important are Damascus, Baghdad and Cairo, which were successively the seats of the four most important Muslim dynasties, the Omayyads, the

Abassids, the Fatimids and the Mamelukes. Then there are Kairouan, Tlemcen, Fez, Meknes, Marrakesh, Cordova and Granada, each of which are associated with one of the glorious periods of Islam and which developed certain aspects of its civilisation to a point which it never matched thereafter.

Above and beyond its theological importance, Mecca is today the urban face of Islam, because these cities are the natural setting for the flowering of the religion, its creative genius and personality.

1. Second holy city of Islam, situated some hundred miles from the Red Sea and two hundred miles north of Mecca.

Mecca in its geographic setting. Nineteenth-century Syrian miniature. Museum of The People's Art, Damascus.

CHAPTER 10

THE KAABA

THE CANONICAL DIRECTION OF EVERY PIOUS ACT, PARTICULARLY PRAYER

THE KAABA IS A CUBE-SHAPED TEMPLE (MUQA'AB) SITUATED IN THE MIDDLE OF THE COURTYARD OF THE GREAT MOSQUE OF MECCA. It is the point at which all the believers converge, and the focus of all spiritual currents.

By virtue of its central position, the Kaaba, called *Bayt Allah al-Haram* (the House of God) or *Bayt al-Haram* (The Sacred House) is the main temple of the Muslim religion. It embodies the divine presence and inspiration.

The Kaaba, which is said to have been built by the patriarch Abraham—and his son Ishmael—is draped in an embroidered cloth (*kiswa*). At one corner is the "Black Stone" which the pilgrims must touch during their pilgrimage.

From this point of view, the Kaaba is truly the earthly *qibla*, the physical lodestone of the Islamic faith and the focus for all the prayers Muslims daily address to their God. In the sura called The Cow, it is written: "Turn then thy face in the direction of the Sacred Mosque: wherever ye are, turn your faces in that direction" (The Cow, II, 144).

The temple is a little over 50 feet high, 33 feet wide and with a 40-foot façade. Six and half feet from the ground, set into an oval frame measuring about 8 inches, is the "Black Stone", the most intimate heart of the shrine.

Legend has it that this was originally a white hyacinth which gradually grew blacker and blacker because of men's sins. The Kaaba owes its power of attraction to this black stone, which passes for the *mithaq*, the "primordial covenant" between the Creator and His creature. Touching it has a profound impact on pilgrims. In fact, it is supposed to count in their favour on the Day of Judgement. When the pilgrim arrives before the Temple, he enters it via the Gateway of Peace before beginning his circumambulation in an anti-clockwise direction. The area situated between the black stone and the door of the temple is called *al-Multazam* and acts as a support to the pilgrims when they are praying.

The great Muslim traveller from Valencia, Ibn Jubayr (1145–1217) describes the emotion he felt on touching the Kaaba: "The stone, when one kisses it, has a softness and freshness which delights the mouth; so much so that he who places his lips upon it wishes never to remove them. [...] It suffices, moreover, that the Prophet said that it is the "Right Hand"[1] of God on Earth."[2]

The Kaaba is covered in a hanging of brocade of black silk, embroidered in gold or silver thread with inscriptions from the Qur'an, which are invocations to God, the *fatiha*, the first sura of the Qur'an, and other verses.

Representation of the Kaaba on ceramic tiles, iznik (Turkey), sixteenth century.
The inscription bottom right reads: Minbar an-Nabi (Pulpit of the Prophet).
Collection of the Louvre Museum, Department of Oriental Antiques.

منبر النبي ﷺ

Once a year, this covering is changed in a symbolic ritual which takes place during the pilgrimage. In ancient times, the highly colourful caravan procession which brought the new covering from Cairo to Mecca was known as the *mahmal*. Egypt was responsible for the temple hanging from the Mameluke period (thirteenth century), before this duty returned to the Wahhabite dynasty of the Beni Saud in 1924. The Wahhabis became the Guardians of the Holy Places by reason of national sovereignty.

The temple itself is made of greyish or greyblue stone from the outskirts of Mecca, and from mortar which came from Yemen. The interior of the Kaaba has also been of great interest for pilgrims and travellers.

Ibn Battuta (1304–1377) gives a lengthy description of it in his account of his voyage (*rihla*): "The interior of the illustrious Kaaba is paved with marbled shaded with white, blue and red: the marble covering its walls is of the same sort. It has three exceedingly high columns made of teak wood and placed four paces apart; they occupy the middle of the space which constitutes the interior of the illustrious Kaaba. The middle one faces the halfway part of the side which is between the two corners of Iraq (Yemen) and Syria."[3]

In 1956, with the growing influx of pilgrims, the immediate surroundings of the Kaaba were removed and a larger, more austere, concourse replaced it. Paving stones were laid, while the pathway between Safa and Marwa, the two holy hillocks, was widened.

When all is said and done, the Kaaba, the place towards which all canonical directions converge, is the epitome of Muslim monotheism. As the embodiment of the unity of the faith, it is also the sign of the unity of Allah and the indissociable link of the Muslim community.

1. *Yamîn*, a word which is difficult to translate, since it has the same etymology as the word "right", as opposed to *shimâl*, which means "left", and thus leads to a possible laterality and hence anthropomorphism of God.
2. Ibn Jubayr, *Voyages*, vol. 1, p. 291. (Paris: Paul Geuthner, 1982).
3. Ibn Battuta, *Voyages*, vol. 1, p. 105. (Paris: La Découverte, 1953–1956).

A pilgrim performing the ritual of kissing the "Black Stone" of the Kaaba at Mecca.

CHAPTER 11

THE QIBLA

THE SPIRITUAL KEY TO ISLAMIC GEOGRAPHY
AND ORIENTATION TOWARDS THE KAABA

THE *QIBLA*, WHICH WAS ESTABLISHED BY THE QUR'AN AS THE RESULT OF A PROLONGED CONTROVERSY WHICH SET THE UNBELIEVERS against the Muslims, symbolises the direction of Mecca of which it is the abstract representation and intense "focalisation".

The initial direction of the *qibla*, established during the Medinan period of the Prophet's life, was towards Jerusalem (622 A.D.) until the revelation of a verse, two years later, which signalled the definitive change of direction: "And we appointed the Qiblah to which thou wast used, only to test those who followed the Messenger from those who would turn on their heels (from the Faith)" (The Cow, II, 143).

Since then, Mecca, the Great Mosque and the Kaaba, which provide the "key" to Islam's spiritual geography, have formed the living centre of Islam. That is why the believers first check the direction in which they are turning before prostrating themselves before God. Once the direction of the *qibla* has been established, earth joins heaven in a sanctified place, the Kaaba, the Sacred Temple of Islam. Animated discussions can often be witnessed between believers in the absence of a mosque and, therefore, of the *mihrab*, which is the architectural symbol of the *qibla* in a

mosque. How should one respond to the dictate of the Qur'an that believers must turn towards Mecca to pray: "We see thee turning thy face (for guidance) to the heavens: now shall we turn thee to a Qiblah that shall please thee. Turn then thy face in the direction of the Sacred Mosque: wherever ye are, turn your faces in that direction" (The Cow, II, 144). This instruction applies to the whole liturgical cycle and is used to attract divine blessings upon a sacrifice, funeral or wedding.

Nevertheless, the "people of the Qibla" (*Ahl al-Qibla*, as the Muslims are called), do not always refer to this precise point, however sacred it is, since, according to the Qur'an, "to Allah belong the East and the West" (The Cow, II, 115). This means that the direction taken matters but little, since Allah is at the beginning and end of all things. "Whithersoever ye turn, there is Allah's countenance", as that same sura says.

In fact, as in the Mosque of Two Qiblas in Medina, the ancient mosque of Qubâ, the very place in which the change of qibla took place, such an orientation has meaning because it epitomises the unity of the centralism of the faith on the one hand and its tolerance on the other: Mecca is not only the centre of the world but it is also in the world.

Qibla compass used, in the absence of a mihrab, to determine the direction in which the pilgrims should turn for prayer. Iran, late nineteenth century. The Nasser D. Khalili Collection of Islamic Art.

CHAPTER 12

THE MOSQUE

THE PLACE OF ASSEMBLY FOR THE COMMUNITY

DESIGNED IN THE IMAGE OF THE FIRST MOSQUE OF THE PROPHET, BUILT IN MEDINA IN THE YEAR 1 A.H. (622 A.D.), THE MOSQUE (*al-jami'*, or *masjid al-jumu'a*) is the place in which Muslims worship collectively. As such, it is the physical symbol of Islam and the place in which collective fervour is expressed.

The mosque plays a much vaster and more complex role than that of a place of worship. In particular, it is the institution in which religious instruction is given, thanks to the colleges housed in its outbuildings, the moral academy in which social activities such as marriage are consecrated and especially, after prayer, the meeting-place in which community life is discussed. It is at the mosque that disputes between Muslims are settled, and also where innovations are considered, rejected or approved. Last but not least, religious authority is expressed and manifested at the mosque, notably during the Friday sermon (*khutba*). The Friday sermon is preached in the great mosque. This is the most important act of devotion since it combines many oratorical talents, such as the visionary skills of the preacher, the exemplary serenity of the pedagogue and the teacher, and the theological talent of the inspired religious leader.

There are several types of mosques, usually classed according to their size and the number of devotees who attend them. The small mosque is called the *musalla* or *masjid*. This is the little chapel in which "prostration" (*sujud*) is performed, Muslims being designated in the Qur'an as "those that bow down and prostrate themselves" (The Repentance, IX, 112). Friday prayers are held in the great mosque. Apart from a large prayer hall and sometimes a sort of mezzanine at the back of the hall set aside for women, the mosque contains the following features:
– the minaret: this is the anglicised form of the Arabic word *manara*, but this most prominent feature of the architecture of the mosque changes its name depending upon the effect the orator wishes to give in his description, and varies from region to region. There is *al-manara*, as just mentioned, but there is also *al-sa'uma*, "the protuberance" or *al-mi'dhana*, "the place in which the call to prayer is raised". The prototype of the minaret is that of the "mosque of Bilal" in Jabal Abu Kobays. Certainly the form is basic, but it also shows the characteristic features of a minaret, especially its extra height. The main function of the minaret, apart from that of balancing the edifice in the aesthetic sense, is to allow the *muezzin* to project his call (*adhân*)

The minbar of the Paris Mosque,
at which the khatib *officiates during his sermons.*

reminding the faithful of the hours of prayer. The minaret is also a symbol of mediation and verticality, which links the mosque to the higher spheres of Muslim cosmology, giving the ritual of kneeling and prostration the sense of a divine flowering of which it is the outward manifestation;

— the *mihrab*: the focal point of the mosque, the hollow alcove in the wall which indicates the direction of Mecca (*qibla*);

— the *minbar*: the preacher's pulpit is part of the ritual furnishings of the mosque. In some great mosques, such as the al-Aqsa Mosque in Jerusalem, this pulpit is magnificently and ornately carved. Although usually made of precious wood, the *minbar* is sometimes modestly represented by a mound or other raised object. The Prophet is even said to have celebrated the Friday sermon perched on the trunk of a palm tree;

— the ablutions hall: before entering the prayer hall, the believer must cleanse himself in thought as well as in deed. It is enjoined upon him to perform his customary ablutions (*wudu'*) in a special room set aside for this purpose and adjoining the mosque, and is an integral part of any mosque. The ablutions hall represents an intermediary space between the profane world of active life and the sacred world of the mosque, a place for meditating, regaining strength and feeling at one with the principles of God, man's Helper. The believer here unloads himself of his major or minor impurities before presenting himself, full of humility, before the Creator.

Aside from the mosques of Mecca and Medina, the most frequented of the Muslim world, several other mosques stand out architecturally:

— The Mosque of Omar or the Al-Aqsa Mosque, and the Dome of the Rock in Jerusalem (late seventh century);

— the university mosque of Al-Azhar (tenth century), in old Cairo, one of the most prestigious in Sunni Islam, since it houses the Academy of Religious Sciences and a High Council of theologians who are highly influential in the fields of Islamic jurisprudence and doctrine;

— the Friday Mosque in Teheran (ninth to eleventh centuries);

— the Quat al-Islam Mosque in Delhi (thirteenth century);

— the Suleymanieh Mosque in Istanbul (fourteenth century);

— the Mezquita of Cordova (eighth to tenth centuries), no longer used for religious purposes;

— the Sidi 'Okba Mosque (twelfth century) in Kairouan, Tunisia, which occupies a place apart since it was the work of 'Okba ibn Nafi', the Muslim general who paved the way for the Islamisation of North Africa. In his honour, Kairouan is sometimes considered the fourth holy city of Islam.

The construction of mosques accompanies the demographic evolution of Islam. Wherever it is situated, the mosque aims to become integrated into the sociological and urban landscape. Through spontaneous mimicry it quite easily accommodates the architectural influences of the country in which it is built. Consider, for example, the red earth mosques of sub-Saharan Africa, those of the Indian sub-continent and of Indonesia, Pakistan and Afghanistan, all of which are distinctive in style.

Preceding double page: Jerusalem, the esplanade of the mosques,
the Mosque of Omar, named after the second Caliph.
Opposite: a believer reading in a mosque in Senegal.

CHAPTER 13

THE MIHRAB

THE COMPASS OF THE MUSLIM WORLD
AND THE MATERIAL REPRESENTATION OF THE *QIBLA*,
THE MIHRAB IS ALSO AN ARCHITECTURAL INNOVATION

THE WORD *MIHRAB* HAS A COMPLEX ETY-MOLOGY (BALCONY, HALL, ROOM) BUT HAS GRADUALLY SHED THESE MULTIPLE MEANINGS and come to mean simply "alcove", "prayer niche" or "apsidiole". It was instituted in the eighth century, most probably in Damascus, when the direction of Mecca (*qibla*) had to be marked on the building of the mosque.

While in exile in Medina, the Prophet had to turn towards the holy city of Jerusalem, but there is no authoritative documentation to show whether the *mihrab* physically existed at that time. Arab historians attribute the initiative of adding a *mihrab* to the mosque to 'Uthman ibn 'Affan, the third Caliph of Islam. However, the *mihrab* only appeared gradually in the format of the mosque, since primitive Islam, apart from not attributing a prominent position to visual symbols such as those found in churches, for example, also shied away from creating them because of the terror this aroused in believers who were used to strict religious orthodoxy.

Yet the Mihrab is a rare example in Islam of a symbol in the fullest sense, since it is the physical representation of the direction of Mecca, which is in itself an abstract concept. Essential to the mosque, the *mihrab* is one symbolic representation which has really spread. It can be seen etched in marble in some decorative wall panels and even on the reverse of the most ancient Islamic coins.

With the development of Islam, the layout of the *mihrab*, and that of the mosque itself have become fundamental to the validity of the prayer offered up therein. The complex requirements for the establishment of the *mihrab* are on a par with the philosophical and theological demands of Islam, a religion which preaches the absolute unity of God. After all, what meaning would a mosque have if it did not face towards Mecca? Arab theologians, architects, mathematicians and astronomers have speculated widely on the possible lines which can and ought to govern the siting and physical representation of the *qibla*. The *mihrab* is the architectural response accepted by the college of Muslim scholars who have studied the matter. Since the eighth to ninth centuries, no deviation from the norm has been tolerated by Muslim doctrine, and mosque-builders' reputations depend upon their following it to the letter.

Several very beautiful *mihrabs* are to be found in the Muslim world. They are the acme of a mosque's refinement. Some are embellished with gold leaf, borders of light and stucco stalactites which give an impression of movement. Others

Mihrab *of the Paris Mosque in classic Moorish style, built in the 1920s.*

are more austere, without any particular additions. Mention is also sometimes made of *mihrabs* made of wood, such as the one in the Tashun Pasha Mosque in Turkey, the construction of which dates back to the thirteenth century. In the opinion of numerous architects, the most remarkable niches are to be found in the following mosques:

− the al-Aqsa Mosque in Jerusalem (eighth century);

− the Great Mosque in Cordova (the Mezquita, tenth century);

− the great mosques of Isfahan and Yazd. The *mihrab* in the former is set in a decor of stucco vegetation (1310), while the latter, dating from 1375, is of glazed earthenware;

− the mausoleum of Sayida˙Rukkayya in Cairo (twelfth century);

− the Konya Mosque (Turkey), with its glazed earthenware *mihrab*, in the Sedrettin Konevi (c. 1274).

Two other such prayer niches are worthy of note because they are among the most original examples of Islamic architecture:

− the Sidi Oqba Mosque in Kairouan (ninth century), the *mihrab* is an excellent example of Arab Islamic art;

− the Ahmad al-Budayni Mosque in Cairo, a *mihrab* which dates from 1628 and has marble inlays in different colours.

Such a list cannot be considered exhaustive, since while experts may agree on the objective history of the building of mosques—and their prayer niches—they disagree on matters of personal taste, so there is no way in which the prayer niches can be ranked in order of artistic merit. On the aesthetic front, the prayer alcove celebrates the art of the craftsmen who devised and designed it, but it is also the expression of a mosque's "personality"; it remains the best reflection of the taste of a particular period and sometimes of the Muslim region in which it is situated.

Certainly without the *mihrab*, the mosque would be a building without magnetisation or liturgical *gravitas*, prey to a sort of spiritual blindness.

Indian mihrab *carved in marble, fourteenth to fifteenth centuries.*
Collection of the Louvre, Department of Oriental Antiques.

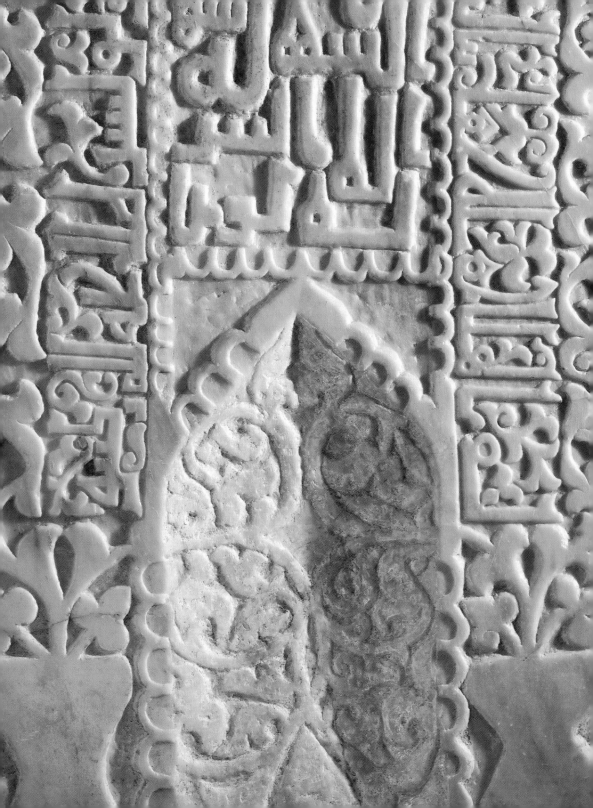

CHAPTER 14

FRIDAY

THE HOLY DAY OF THE MUSLIM WEEK

FRIDAY IS THE "DAY OF GATHERING" OR "ASSEMBLY". IT IS THUS CALLED BECAUSE OF THE CONGREGATIONAL PRAYER WHICH IS said in the great mosque as soon as the sun has passed the meridian. It is a holy day for Muslims. The Qur'an mentions the Friday prayer only once, in the sura entitled Friday: "O ye who believe! When the call is proclaimed to prayer on Friday (The Day of Assembly), hasten earnestly to the remembrance of Allah, and leave off business (and traffic): that is best for you if ye but knew!" (Friday, LXII, 9).

Es-Said ben Yazîd, the source of numerous oral traditions, relates that "in the time of the Prophet, the first call to prayer on a Friday came when the imam took the pulpit. It was also thus under the Caliphs 'Abu-Bakr and 'Umar. 'Uthman ordained a third call to prayer during his caliphate as the population had grown. This call was made at Ez-Zawira (a district of Medina). This dictate was later kept up."[1]

It should be recalled at this juncture that, as in most elements of the dogma, the Friday prayer was codified at the time of the four first Caliphs, who have been dubbed *al-Khulafa al-Rashidun* (the Properly-Guided Caliphs), those same men who had

accompanied the Prophet in his many battles against the hostility and wrongdoings of the idolators.

The Friday prayer (*salât al-jumu'a*), upon which the entire spiritual and esoteric significance of that day is structured, is an act of great blessedness for all Muslims who can reach the great mosque. A ceremonial call (*adhân*) is raised by the *muezzin*, but a great number of Muslims are already in their places because they attend the mosque very early in the morning.

According to Abu-Horayra, a companion of the Prophet, Muhammad said: "When Friday comes, the angels are standing at the door of the mosque. They note the first comer, and the second (and so on). He who comes early is like a man who gives alms of a fat camel, and then (successively) a man who gives alms of a bull, then a ram, then a chicken, then an egg. When the *imam* comes out, the angels shut their registers and listen to the mention of God."[2]

Because it is congregational and gathers the whole community in the mosque (*jami'*), the Friday prayer is undoubtedly the most important of the week. It is accompanied by an important instructive and moral sermon (*khutba*) given by

Believers entering the mosque for the Friday prayer.

the *imam* on behalf of the religious authority of the land and hence on behalf of Islam as a whole.

This is how Ibn Abî Zayd al-Qayrawâni (tenth century) described the rite as it was observed in mâlikism, one of the four canonical schools of the Sunnis, found mainly in North Africa, black Africa and a part of Egypt: "The Friday prayer is obligatory in an urban centre and in a group of believers forming a community. The sermon is obligatory before the prayer itself. The *imam* must lean on a bow or a stick and sit down at the beginning and in the middle (of the *khutba*). The prayer begins when the sermon is ended. [...] Those in the town or within a radius of three miles or less from it must hasten to the Friday prayer. It is not obligatory for travellers, pilgrims at Minâ, slaves, women or children who have not attained puberty. But if a slave or a woman are present at the prayer, they should observe it. Women are placed behind the rows of men. The *imam* who is giving the sermon must be attentively listened to, and the believers should face him."[3]

Having realised the influence of the Friday prayer on the believers, the great dynasties—and later the Muslim states, the best example of which is Saudi Arabia—have done their utmost to control the occasion, by building more and more imposing mosques intended to admit the largest number of believers. Although Friday is a public holiday in many Muslim countries, unlike the Lord's day of rest as mentioned in Genesis[4] it does not correspond to a possible rest from creation. The Qur'an clearly stipulates in the sura Qâf that: "We created the heaven and the earth and all

between them in Six Days, nor did any sense of weariness touch Us" (L, 38).

On a symbolic level, Friday is the pivot of the week and consequently of the liturgical time. It therefore has the same position in time as the mosque occupies in space.

1. El-Bokhari, vol. 1, p. 299.
2. *Ibid.*, p. 303.
3. Al-Qayrawâni, *La Risâla*, p. 95.
4. Genesis (I: 31).

Believers praying in front of the Ketchaona Mosque, Algeria.

CHAPTER 15

IMAM AND MUEZZIN

THE *MUEZZIN*, *KHATIB* AND *IMAM*, THE THREE MAIN FIGURES WHO LEAD THE PRAYER

PERCHED ON TOP OF THE MINARET (*AL-MANARA*), THE *MUEZZIN*, FROM THE ARABIC WORD *AL-MUADHDHÎN*, IS RESPONSIBLE FOR calling the faithful to worship in the mosque. It is a canonical duty instituted by the Prophet himself and implemented in the first mosque of Islam, built in Medina the Enlightened (*al-Munawara*).

The Abyssinian Bilal, who had been a slave of Abu-Bakr as-Saddiq (570–634), one of the Prophet's closest companions, took on this function. It is one of the most important functions in the ritual. Since the seventh century, the *muezzin*, an officiant specially trained in vocal technique, has been raising a call to prayer, his hand cupping his mouth. The call consists of seven very specific phrases:

– *Allahu Akbar, Allahu Akbar*: "God is Most Great, God is Most Great";
– *Ash-hadu anna Muhammad rasul Allah*: "I testify that Muhammad is the Prophet of God" (twice);
– *Haya 'ala as-salat, haya 'ala as-salat*: "Come to prayer" (twice);
– *Haya 'ala al-falah, haya 'ala al-falah*: "Come to salvation or deliverance" (twice);
– *Allahu Akbar*: "God is Most Great" (twice);
– *La ilaha ilal-Lah*: "There is no god but God".

There is a variation in the dawn prayer, since the *muezzin* twice repeats, for the benefit of those who, tempted into error by Satan, would prefer to carry on sleeping: "Prayer is more meritorious than sleep" (*As-salât khayru mina-nawm*) before pronouncing the final formula. The importance of this call (*adhân*) stems from the spiritual value of all congregational prayers, which are twenty-seven times better than individual prayers.

The *khatib* or preacher is often a theologian of renown, a high-ranking emissary or a scholar from within the Muslim community, with a fund of incontestable knowledge. His primary function is to deliver a sermon known as the *khutba*, at the Friday prayer. Usually, he will be seated on a raised platform or high chair called a *minbar* and placed on the right (from the believers' point of view) of the *mihrab*.

The role of the Khatib is principally religious and theological, which explains the multitude of Qur'anic quotations and references to the Islamic era. He does, however, also have to deal with general knowledge or social, political and juridical issues.

In the past, the caliphate held considerable influence over the ideological orientation of the Friday sermon. There was even a time when this

Muezzin calling the believers to prayer.

function was the prerogative of the ruling family or its appointed representatives, whether they were a *qadi* (religious judge), an *'alam* (theologian) or even a *talib* (advanced student of religious knowledge). Today, political regimes try to stamp the exercise with their own mark of legitimacy and popularity, with varying degrees of success.

After having been summoned by the *muezzin* and having listened to the preacher's sermon, Muslims are invited to stand and perform the great prayer, the leadership of which is entrusted to an *imam*, literally "he who stands in front (of the others)".[1] The *imam*, who stands in the arch of the *mihrab*, is an important figure because he conducts and regulates the mechanics of the congregational prayer, while assuring its validity in the eyes of God. He is chosen from among healthy Muslims (who are free men, particularly in the time of the Prophet), preferably of sound physical constitution and possessing a sufficient level of knowledge and proven skills. In small mosques, the *imam* may also be the *khatib* (preacher); sometimes the same person performs the functions of *muezzin*, *khatib* and *imam*.

On the spiritual front, the *imam* must set a good example. He also sometimes intervenes between the Muslim and the institution, either in matters of theological exegesis connected with the dogma or in personal matters. The *imam* also intervenes in the various disputes between Muslims outside the context of worship and helps them to concentrate their minds, thus contributing to the permanent process of education so characteristic of Islam.

In leading the congregation in prayer, these three figures, the *muezzin*, the *khatib* and the *imam*, are responsible for religious services which take place five times a day.

Insofar as the Friday prayer is very well-attended, it provides the *muezzin* and the *khatib* with the opportunity of expressing the whole range of their talents: in the case of the *muezzin*, he should have a strong, musical voice which is pleasing to the ear; the sermon of the *khatib* should be creative and inspired, while the prayer should be lead in a measured and modulated manner.

1. In the ninth century, the word *imam* was endowed with a new meaning. While for Sunnis it is only one term among others which is applied to anyone who leads the collective prayer, *imam* for Shi'ites is a religious title pertaining to several high dignitaries. This theological and religious hierarchy is structured around the advent of the twelfth *Imam*, the hidden *Imam* who will close, at the end of time, the cycle inaugurated and embodied by the eleven other *Imams*.

Minaret of the Paris Mosque in classic Moorish style (first quarter of the twentieth century).

CHAPTER 16

THE MADRASSA

THE INSTITUTION IN WHICH ISLAMIC KNOWLEDGE IS TAUGHT AND ACQUIRED, AND A PLACE OF CONVIVIALITY

ONE OF THE MAIN CONTRIBUTIONS OF ISLAM WAS TO ENCOURAGE ACCESS TO LEARNING, ESPECIALLY RELIGIOUS LEARNING. There is no barrier between those who know and those who do not yet know, between scholars (*talib*) and the object of their quest. There are three different degrees of knowledge in Islam:

– Allah is the All-Knowing, He Whose knowledge encompasses the manifest and the hidden, the great mystery of the Universe which mystics call by the term *al-ghayb*. The Qur'an reminds the reader of this immeasurable knowledge and makes it one of the branches of divine truth: "Enough for a witness between me and you is Allah, and such as have knowledge of the Book" (The Thunder, XIII, 43). The concept of the "knowledge of God" (*'ilm Allah*) is given numerous interpretations (God knows everything, even the mystery of the hour of the Final Judgement; he is perfectly informed of people's actions, their good deeds or their misdeeds, their thoughts, etc.), in over three hundred verses of the Qur'an and almost all the suras;

– the knowledge of the Prophet Muhammad is an extension of the knowledge of prophecy inaugurated by Adam, the first Prophet recognised in Islam. As the repository of the most recent monotheistic religion, Muhammad possesses the thousand and one facets of belief and faith from all time. He himself had preached for the benefit of his supporters and followers that knowledge should be sought even if this meant travelling as far afield as China. These words of the Prophet are regarded as authentic because they have been reported by several compilers of traditions, the most eminent of whom is El-Bokhari (810–870) and, in the same century, Muslim (817–875);

– a third category of those with knowledge consists of Muslim scholars and sages, whether they are well-versed in the field of the Islamic sciences, know the Qur'an by heart, interpret it or seek to resolve social and interpersonal conflicts by specialising in Islamic jurisprudence (*fiqh*). Those engaged in more "intellectual" disciplines such as grammar, historiography, rhetoric and all the speculative disciplines such as logic and philosophy which Muslims refer to collectively as *'ilm al-kalam*, also belong in this category.

It is within this context that one can place the rise and dazzling efflorescence of the *madrassa*, "the place of learning", from the verb *darassa*, "to study", and *darrassa*, "to teach". Here the tradition of learning in Islam is perpetuated, especially as regards the Qur'an and the *hadith*. These school-universities can legitimately claim their spiritual ancestry from

*Reading and copying the Qur'an
are the two principal activities in the* madrassa.

two illustrious institutions: the Bayt al-Hikma, the Abbasid "House of Wisdom" built in Baghdad in the ninth century;[1] and the Fatimid university-mosque of Al-Azhar, founded in 972 A.D. in Cairo, a city also built by the Fatimids in 969.

In practice, the madrassa, or médersa as it is known in North Africa, is not solely a place for lessons and long hours of Qur'anic recitation (activities performed in the mosque with greater efficiency and comfort), it is above all a focus of life for all the many students who attend it, some of whom come from the most far-flung regions of the Muslim world.

Each great mosque has an adjoining madrassa, and some are so beautiful and famous that they have acquired a universal reputation.

This is the case with the Nuriya madrassa in the Khawasin quarter of Damascus, built in 1167 and described by Ibn Jubayr (twelfth century): "One of those in this world which afford the most beautiful sight to the eyes is that of the late Nur-Ad-Dîn, where his tomb lies. May God illuminate him! It is a most magnificent palace: water flows there, first descending into a channel in the middle of a large waterway, then flowing into an oblong fountain and finally falling into an ornamental pool in the middle of the building. The eyes are amazed by the beauty of this spectacle. All those who see it reiterate their prayers for Nur-ad-Dîn."[2] The magnificence of the Moroccan médersas is also remarkable, especially those of Fez or Marrakesh (the fourteenth-century Al-Attarine médersa; the fourteenth-century Bou Inania médersa; the seventeenth-century Esh-Sher-ratin médersa).

With the mosque and as a complement to the madrassa, one should also mention the zawiya, the sanctuary which houses the shrine of a saint. A building characteristic of North African Islam, the zawiya passes on a popular heritage and memory of Islam. The Qur'an and the disciplines ensuing from it are usually taught there.

Even the modest buildings of country zawiyas can also be used as mosques. This accentuates its image as a para-Islamic or even heretical sanctuary, taking into account of the practices which sometimes take place there.

1. Though it was Nizam al-Mulk (eleventh century), the powerful Vizir of the Sultan Malik Shah, who gave it its impetus.
2. Ibn Jubayr, Voyages, vol. 3, p. 330.

Preceding double page and opposite:
"He who follows the path to knowledge,
God will smooth his path to Paradise" (hadith of the Prophet).

CHAPTER 17

HOLY DAYS AND RITUALS

THE *HIJRA* IS THE BASIS OF THE MUSLIM CALENDAR, WHILE THE LUNAR YEAR PROVIDES THE RHYTHM FOR THE LIFE OF BELIEVERS

THE RITES OF BIRTH, PROTECTION AND DEATH ARE A SKILFUL BLEND OF CUSTOMS AND RELIGIOUS DICTATES. IN DAILY LIFE, Muslims do not believe in any power besides Allah, but in moments of confusion they sometimes have recourse to talismans to guard them from the evil eye and from the *jettatura*.[1] These amulets contain Qur'anic verses and recall the authority of God over Satan.

Rites and prohibitions pertaining to food are especially important. The Muslim dietary laws are rigorously codified. Works on theology and jurisprudence go into minute details concerning the thousand and one situations—medical, purifying, sacrificial—in which meat acquires the status of *halal*, or conversely, make it unfit for consumption. Food prohibitions extend to permitted types of meat from an animal not specifically slaughtered in the name of Allah, or which has not been caught expressly for the purpose of consumption. "Forbidden to you (for food) are dead meat, blood, the flesh of swine, and that on which hath been invoked the name of other than Allah; that which hath been killed by strangling, or by a violent blow, or by a headlong fall, or by being gored to death; that which hath been (partly) eaten by a wild animal, unless ye are able to slaughter it (in due form); that which is sacrificed on stone (altars)" (The Repast, V, 3). A similar ban is placed on intestines and carrion, since it is written that "It is not their meat nor their blood that reaches Allah" (The Pilgrimage, XXII, 37).

As for sacrifice and immolation, part of the ancient Arab heritage, these are reinforced and confirmed in the Qur'an: "We have placed sacrificial animals among those things which are sacred to Allah: in them there is much good for you: then pronounce the name of Allah over them as they are made ready for slaughter: when they are lying down on their sides (after slaughter), eat ye thereof, and feed such as (beg not but) live in contentment, and such as beg with due humility" (The Pilgrimage, XXII, 36). In Islam, the most important of sacrificial rituals is the slaughter of an animal—a sheep, camel, bull or goat. This is how Muslims commemorate Abraham's act when, following divine injunctions, he would have sacrificed his son Ishmael. The feast commemorating the act, the Feast of Sacrifice (*'Id al-Adha*), is called the *'Id al-Kabir* (Great Feast) to distinguish

Calendar on a roll of parchment inscribed with the times of Muslim prayer in each month of the solar year and other important events in the religious year. Turkey, early nineteenth century. The Nasser D. Khalili Collection of Islamic art.

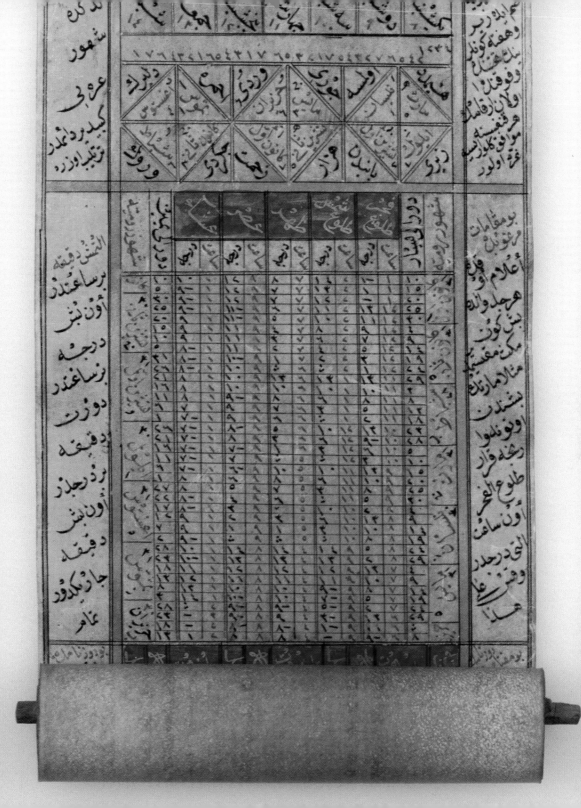

it from the feast which falls at the end of Ramadan. It takes place on the tenth day of the month of pilgrimage (*Dhu'l-Hijja*). Muslim (816–873) reports the following words attributed to the Prophet: "When you slaughter an animal, slaughter it in an excellent fashion: let each one of you sharpen his blade and not mistreat the animal he is about to sacrifice."[2]

In order that the meat should be permitted (*halal*), the person performing the sacrifice—any adult Muslim in a state of canonical purity and practised in the field of sacrifice—follows very precise ritual instructions: to turn in the direction of Mecca, invoke the name of Allah and slit the animal's throat deftly, without, however, separating the head from the body. Some animals are unfit for consumption. These include dogs, cats, wolves, foxes, wild boars and pigs. The same applies to the raven, because of the bad omens associated with it, and some birds of prey. As they feed on human flesh, eating them could create precedents of cannibalism.

Muslim religious judges advise against their consumption. In Europe, meat is supervised by the veterinary services of the great mosque This festival of sacrifice, the *'Id al-Kabir*, is certainly not the only one. It is part of the wider framework of Arab and Muslim dietary laws which still play a part in some popular beliefs.

The rite of circumcision also occupies a very important place. Although the Qur'an does not contain any references to it, circumcision (*khitan*) is a Bedouin and Semitic practice highly recommended for male children. It has gradually come to

occupy a place in the rituals of the Muslim world, especially in the central regions (Iran, Turkey, Egypt, Arabia, Muslim Africa and North Africa). Circumcision has emerged as a collective tradition symbolising a form of perfection, but not as a substitute for faith. Circumcision corresponds as much to religious as to medical, hygienic and social requirements. According to region, it is performed when a child is between three and nine years of age. Nowadays, the tendency is to make it as painless as possible by advocating it at an early age and having it performed by a paediatrician or surgeon in properly sterile conditions.

Rituals reinforce the adherence and respect of a Muslim for his religion. They are a source of dogma and law, but also a method of differentiating between beliefs, as expressed in the Qur'an: "To every people did We appoint rites (of sacrifice) that they might celebrate the name of Allah" (The Pilgrimage, XXII, 34). And as they relay identity to millions of people, rituals are the focus for a spiritual revival in religious life.

Other important events in religious life are the feasts which punctuate the Muslim year. The Muslim calendar (or the era of the *Hijra*) is built on the lunar year. It officially began on 24 September 622 A.D., which corresponds to the twelfth day of *Rabi'al-awwal* in the year 1 A.H.[3] The word *hijra* means "exile", "emigration" or "expatriation"; thus, the Muslim year can be seen to be the advent of a new cycle and not just the leftovers of the pagan calendar of pre-Islamic Hijaz. This exodus occurred on 16 September 622, when, persecuted by their Meccan enemies, the Prophet and his companions emigrated to Yathrib, as Medina was then called. Medina thus became the refuge of the Islamic community, the place in which the new faith was adopted, and the first city-state. The Muslim year is a lunar year consisting of twelve months, which are twenty-nine or thirty days long. It has 355 or 356 days, a difference of about eleven days from the solar year, hence the annual gap between the Hegirian and the Gregorian calendars. The names of the Muslim months are as follows: *Muharram, Safar, Rabi'al-awwal, Rabi' al-thani, Jumada al-ula, Jumada al-thaniya, Rajab, Sha'ban, Ramadan, Shawwal, Dhu'l-Qa'da, Dhu'l-Hijja*. Four holy months are mentioned in the Qur'an and are called "months of God":

– *Muharram* (literally forbidden, prohibited, and thus, holy), is the first month of the Muslim year;

– *Rajab* is a month which was venerated even before the advent of Islam;

– *Dhu'l-Qa'da*, which means "the month of rest", is the eleventh month of the year. It is a month of truce, in which rival clans suspend their conflicts and attend to their trading occupations;

– *Dhu'l-Hijja* is the twelfth month of the Muslim year and the month of pilgrimage to Mecca.

There are many other feasts and ceremonies which mark the Muslim year:

I. THE NEW YEAR (*Ras al-'am*), 1 *Muharram*. This is the start of the Muslim calendar. Iranians, however, remain attached to Naw-Ruz (literally "New Light"), the Sassanid new year which survived the advent of Islam and is celebrated at the vernal equinox (21 March).

II. 'ASHURA, 10 *Muharram*. On this day, many Muslims fast, pray and perform ritual activities. For Shi'ites, it has a different significance, since this lucky day is a day of national mourning. In fact, 'Ashura recalls the painful memory of the death of Hussein, the second son of the Imam 'Ali, which took place on 10 *Muharram* 680 at Karbala' (Iraq).

III. THE BIRTH OF THE PROPHET (*Mawlid an-Nabi*), 12 *Rabi' al-awwal*. During this birthday feast, which is widely celebrated in the Muslim world, mystic prayers and readings of the Qur'an are organised. In North Africa, it is called *al-Mouled*.

IV. THE NIGHT OF THE PROPHETS ASCENSION INTO HEAVEN (*Laylat al-mi'raj*), 27 *Rajab*. According to hagiographic accounts, this took place during the second year of the Prophet's dispensation. Although it is not greatly celebrated by believers, the night of the Prophet's ascension is propitious for meetings of meditation and invocation of God, at which ritual libations are also offered.

V. THE NIGHT OF POWER, ALSO CALLED THE NIGHT OF THE DECREE (*Laylat al-Qadr*), 27 *Ramadan*. This is the most important night of the month, being the night of the revelation of the Qur'an: "We have indeed revealed this (Message) in the Night of Power" (The Night of Power, XCVII,1). Spiritually, it is worth a thousand nights together, and the Qur'an defines it as a night of "Peace [...] until the rise of Morn" (The Night of Power, XCVII, 5).

VI. THE FEAST OF THE BREAKING OF THE FAST (*'Id al-fitr*), also called the "Lesser Feast" (*'Id al-saghir*), 1 *Shawwal*. It owes its importance to the fact that it brings to a close the month of the annual fast. It is celebrated on 1 *Shawwal*, the following month. An important prayer performed at the mosque marks the beginning of the celebrations which sometimes last two or three days.

VII. THE FEAST OF THE SACRIFICE (*'Id al-adha*), 10 *Dhu'l-Hijja*. This is also known as the "Great Feast" (*Kurban bayram*, in Turkey), commemorating as it does the sacrifice of Abraham. Donation and sharing are its essence. It is within this strictly religious framework that the slaughter of the 'Id sheep takes place. Once it has been sacrificed and carved into portions, it is meant to be distributed to the family, the poor and friends. This is also true for those who are in Mecca for the pilgrimage. Their sheep is sacrificed in the prescribed places, and surplus meat shared out among the poor.

To this calendar of rituals should also be added other social and family occasions such as marriage (*zawaj*) or the completion of a Qur'anic apprenticeship (*khatma*). Marriage, for instance, demands the active and complete participation of the whole family, and sometimes even the whole clan. The standing of marriage in Islamic lands is so high that even very poor families sometimes hold week-long banquets, although doing so may mean incurring heavy debts. Its religious significance arises from the rejection of celibacy in Islam: Muslims follow the example of the Prophet and his close companions, who constantly praised marriage. Qur'anic apprenticeship, meanwhile, follows rules of a pedagogical order and of the transmission of memory. It begins in early childhood in the nearest Qur'anic school, and continues until university. Theoretically, *khatma* involves those who have learnt the whole Qur'an by heart, but families are delighted if their children have managed to learn only half or three quarters. Often the culmination of this training is celebrated with a meal to which the whole family is invited.

1. A note should, however, be added here on a characteristic object of Arab folklore: the hand of Fatima. This is as widespread as horseshoes which are hung on the pediments of doors to ward off curses, or the drawings of fish in fishing villages. The hand of Fatima is a social symbol going back particularly to popular Arab-Berber culture, but does not correspond to any ritual, Qur'anic or traditional dictates.

2. Nawawi, *Les Quarante Hadiths*, p. 46. (Paris: Les Deux Océans, 1980).

3. In fact, the decision to make the new calendar start at the time of the Hijra goes back to Omar, the second Caliph. Historians date this decision to the year 17 A.H., that is, 639 A.D.

Stamp of halal, *which must be shown on all permitted meat eaten by Muslims.*

CHAPTER 18

POSTURES AND BEHAVIOUR

SOBRIETY GOVERNS ALL THE ACTIONS OF A MUSLIM

MUSLIM THEOLOGIANS BELIEVE THAT IN ORDER TO BE IDENTIFIED AND VALIDATED, BELIEF MUST ENTAIL A SERIES OF SIGNIFICANT acts which make it visible to oneself and to others.

This behaviour involves social and individual conduct. Manner of dress, prayer, the cut of the hair and the nails, the wearing of the veil by women, and personal hygiene. Abu-Horayra (seventh century) recounts that the Prophet Muhammad had said that five acts were recommended for Muslims apart from those ordained in the Qur'an, or the *sunna*: circumcision, shaving the pubic and armpit hair for women, cutting one's nails and trimming one's moustache.

Islam is thus replete with actions which distinguish it, indisputably, from the other great monotheistic religions, Judaism and Christianity, but also from Buddhism, Shintoism, animist religions, Shamanism, and finally, from the American Indian religions.

— The body and prayer: the most obvious external aspect of Muslim prayer is the many postures which the body successively takes up: leaning forward, kneeling, prostration, standing upright, gestures of hailing Allah and blessing Him, etc. Stretching out the index finger—the finger of the profession of faith (*shahada*) is required at the end

of every Muslim prayer. All these gestures proceed from the Qur'anic injunction of humility (*khushu'*), which appears numerous times in the Qur'an (seventeen times about the first prostration) and the prototype of which could be this verse from the sura Al-Fath: "Thou wilt see them bow and prostrate themselves (in prayer), seeking Grace from Allah and (His) Good Pleasure. On their faces are their marks, (being) the traces of their prostration" (The Victory, XLVIII, 29).

Bowing down and prostrating oneself serve to characterise Muslims, since it is said that they are those who "bow down and prostrate themselves" (The Repentance, IX, 112). Through this obedience, they oppose Iblis, the archetype of the devil in Islam, who refused to prostrate himself, as recounted in the Holy Book: "And behold, we said to the angels, 'Bow down to Adam': and they bowed down: not so Iblis: he refused and was haughty: he was of those who reject the Faith" (The Cow, II, 34).

— Hygiene: Islam's attitude to bodily cleanliness (*tahara, nadhafa*) is linked to faith according to a very famous saying of the Prophet: "Cleanliness is inextricably linked to faith."[1] The entire Islamic philosophy of bathing and ablutions, major or minor, as well as that of the general hygiene of the

Attitude of a person invoking Allah in prayer for a simple blessing (du'a).

believer, springs from this precept. This is also true for the *hammam*, the baths, which are the pivot of two complementary worlds, the sacred world of the mosque and the profane world of the exchange, the street, the *souk*, etc. Fragrance and cleanliness are recommended in every case, even if—the odour of sanctity being binding!—"the stench of the mouth of he who is fasting is more pleasing to God than the odour of musk."[2]

The length of hair and nails is codified. The Prophet wore a beard which, it is said, could fit into the palm of the hand without going beyond the base of the neck (*tolia*). He cleaned it, smoothed it and perfumed it. Since then the length of the beard and, even more, the moustache, have become conditions of hygiene encouraged by Islam. Since excess is frowned upon, in this matter as in all others, a beard which reaches the chest is not considered a sign of greater virtue. Nails must be cut and kept clean. According to the very words of the Prophet, reported by Abu Horayra, and subsequently by El-Bokhari, depilation and shaving of the female pubic hair is encouraged, as is a suitable hairstyle.
– Prohibitions: other than pork and all other meat not sacrificed in the name of Allah, Islam forbids the drinking of all alcoholic beverages, even if the alcohol content is negligible. Thus, for example, aperitifs, wines, cakes containing the merest hint of alcohol, chocolates, syrups and stews containing a sprinkling, a dash or a drop of any wine or spirit, even a residue, are forbidden. Islam also forbids gambling, condemns illicit gains, games of forfeiture and usury, and disap-

proves of winnings from gambling at the lottery, the casino, etc. These prohibitions come from a Qur'anic dictate: "They ask thee concerning wine and gambling. Say: 'In them is great sin, and some profit, for men; but the sin is greater than the profit'" (The Cow, II, 219).

The avowed intent of Islam is to allow the individual to have mastery of his own free will, since in freedom of choice there lies the great risk that the Muslim will abandon the most basic religious duties in favour of gaming and its "satanic allures".

1. *Hadith* of the Prophet.
2. *Hadith* reported by El-Bokhari, vol. 4, p. 127.

Woman prostrating herself in prayer.

CHAPTER 19

PRAYER BEADS

MISBAHA: THE ENDLESS RECITATION OF THE NAME OF ALLAH

THE RECITATION OF THE NINETY-NINE FULL NAMES OF ALLAH USING THE PRAYER-BEADS (SUBHA OR MISBAHA) IS an old mnemonic practice used in every Muslim country. The symbolism connected with the prayer beads is that of the "chain of worlds". A discreet reference to sacred numerology is also contained therein, as the symbolism of numbers permeates the activity of the meditator.

Custom dictates that litanies called wird[1] should be recited with devotion and in a continuous manner, the beads having the purpose of aiding concentration and rhythm and punctuating the exercise. More traditional formulas such as the shahada, which recalls the unity of God, and tahmid, thanksgiving to Allah for His blessings, are also said on the beads. The compound structure of the prayer beads (three sections of thirty-three beads each) contributes to its particular spiritual significance. There are also rosaries with thirty-three beads which are used to complete the prayer cycle. For Islam, the beads number ninety-nine and correspond to the beautiful names of Allah, al-asma al-husna, the hundredth attribute being absolute mystery.

In fact, this hundredth figure only appears to be missing, since the two ends of the rosary join up in a sort of long horn which symbolises the name of Allah. However, theologians remain divided as to this explanation, and some reject the idea that the essence of God the Creator should be reduced to this appendage.

The exact origin of the prayer beads is unknown, but the custom was probably introduced by the Sufi movements of the first two centuries of Islam, inspired by distant Indo-Iranian origins. Long sessions of meditation (zikr) indeed involve prayers which require the use of the rosary.

The prayer beads have become a visible reality in Muslim cities. Some believers are never parted from them. They are often made of wood, but can also be fashioned from more precious materials, such as onyx or ivory. While expressing the believer's attachment to his faith, the use of the prayer beads serves to reinforce the belief of the faithful and their constant self-perfection.

---

1. "Glorified be God, Praised be God, Allah is Most Great" (Subhan Allah, Al-Hamduli'llah, Allahu Akbar).

There are two main types of prayer beads, consisting of ninety-nine or thirty-three beads.

CHAPTER 20

CLOTHING

SIGN OF DECENCY AND ADHERENCE TO THE SPIRIT OF THE FAITH

WHEN DRESSING, ESPECIALLY FOR FEASTS OR TO GO TO THE MOSQUE, MUSLIMS FAVOUR LONG WHITE TUNICS (QAMIS) WHICH COVER their shape and at the same time protect them from the intense heat.

The turban and skull-cap, the traditional headcoverings of the Islamic world, fulfil the same function. For town wear, extensive use is made of delicate materials such as cotton, linen and silk; in the country, clothes are rougher and wool is more widely used. The origin of the term *turban* is unclear, since each country has its own name for it. In Algeria, the word *a'mamâ* is preferred, while in Tunisia and Egypt the term *tarbouche* is used. The turban, which is reserved for Muslim dignitaries, has adopted very different shapes according to the various Muslim regions, especially at the time when a united Islam welded together vast areas of the globe. Indeed, the often successful marriage of the turban and the Ottoman fez, the Sassanid tiara, the Moghul skullcap, the Targhi *litham* and the North African tarboosh, all used to cover or wrap the head, facilitated the emergence and preservation of a specificity of local dress and accessories. This is equally true of Islam in Asia, Africa or the Balkans, and even of Almohad Andalusia, where a mutual tolerance can be observed between so-called Arab dress and some elements of the Iberian costume.

From the nineteenth century onwards, under the influence of colonisation, the custom of dressing in European style spread. Clothing in Islam is like an index of the vitality of the religion, since, like religious architecture (mosques, mausoleums, *madrasas*), it has taken root in some newly-Islamicised regions.

Ideally, women should veil themselves whenever they leave their homes, whether to go to the mosque or to attend to their errands. This is an important Qur'anic precept which can tolerate no exception.

Wearing the veil[3] is for women a manifestation of virtue: "Say to the believing women that they should lower their gaze and guard their modesty; that they should not display their beauty and ornaments except what (must ordinarily) appear thereof; that they should draw their veils over their bosoms and not display their beauty except to their husbands, their fathers, their husbands' fathers, their sons, their husbands' sons, their brothers or their brothers' sons, or their sisters' sons, or their women, or their slaves whom their right hands possess, or male servants free of physical needs, or small children" (The Light, XXIV, 31).[1]

Opposite: the skull-cap is the traditional male headcovering during prayer.
Following double page: traditional North African dress;
left, Moroccan dress; right, clothing worn in Kabylia (Algeria).

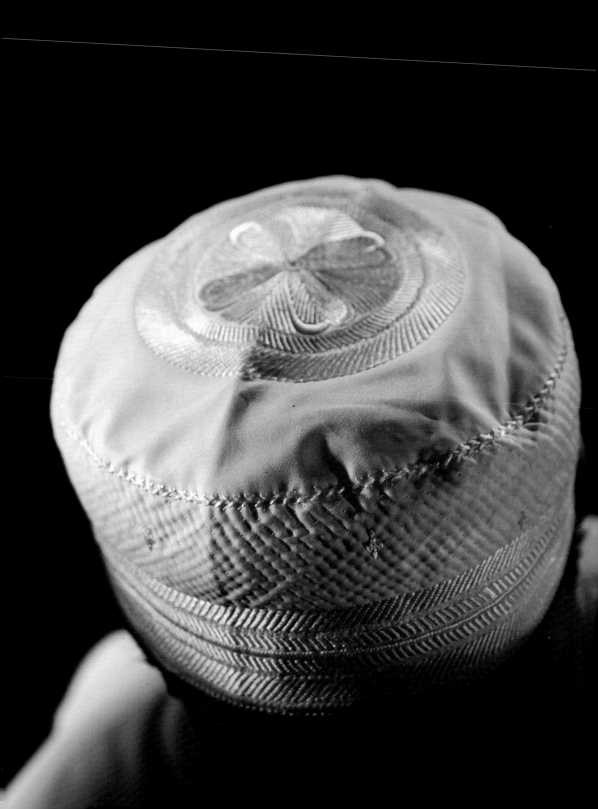

In the seventh century, the veil characterised the Prophet's harem; it was a sign of distinction, by which a woman of good birth sought to show that she was virtuous: "O Prophet! Tell thy wives and daughters, and the believing women, that they should cast their outer garments over their persons (when abroad): that is most convenient that they should be known (as such) and not molested" (The Confederates, XXXIII, 59). Later, in the time of the Egyptian Mamelukes, between 1258 and 1512, the veil, which had always symbolised social distinction, was particularly favoured by the women of Cairo.

The veil defines the limits of a person's inviolability, especially that of a woman, since it is less a case of segregating women (a new concept) than of symbolising their modesty and respectability. On the question of the veil, the official attitude of Muslim countries is very wide-ranging.

Countries such as Iran, the Sudan and, more recently, Afghanistan, enforce the wearing of the veil, while others, such as Egypt or Algeria, accept it with greater difficulty. Still others, such as Tunisia, openly fight it. Women in Arabia, Yemen and other countries of the Gulf have been wearing veils for a long time, without it ever seeming strange or open to exegesis.

In France, where it is a sign of the way in which Muslim women are different, the veil is still the subject of controversy, while in the United Kingdom, for example, it is much better tolerated. Whether or not the veil is universally worn is often a reflection of the tone set by the leadership of existing parties, especially when Muslims are in individual or collective contact with lay circles, in which women are traditionally unveiled. A similar problem arises concerning co-education. While it is absolutely prohibited in the Muslim world, it is considered a social norm in European countries.

At all times and in all places, the function of clothing is to ensure sobriety, decency and modesty. Ibn 'Abbas (seventh century), a companion of the Prophet, said: "Eat whatever you please and wear any clothes you wish, as long as you do not commit either of two things: prodigality or parsimony."

1. The veil is called by different names in different countries: *litham* in the Arab world, *chador* in Iran and *chadi* in Afghanistan, *charshaf* in Turkey, *safsari* in Tunisia, *hijab*, *hayq* in Algeria, etc.

The wearing of the veil is a Qur'anic duty for women. It may be made of different materials and its colour varies from country to country.

CHAPTER 21

WATER

THE SOURCE OF LIFE AND AN IMPORTANT
ELEMENT IN RITUAL

IN ISLAM, WATER, MORE THAN ANY OTHER ELEMENT, IS BLESSED, BECAUSE IT IS THE SPRING THAT FLOODS MAN WITH ITS DIVINE providence and favour: "And We send down from the sky rain charged with blessing, and We produce therewith gardens and grain for harvests; and tall (and stately) palm trees, with shoots of fruit stalks, piled one over another—as sustenance for (Allah's) servants" (Qaf, L, 9–11).

Water has various origins and functions. There is the water for ablutions, water from the well of Zamzam, water from the caravan water-skins, water from the well and the oasis, water from fountains and taps.

In the sura entitled The Prophets, it is written: "Do not the unbelievers see that the heavens and the earth were joined together (as one unit of creation) before we clove them asunder? We made from water every living thing. Will they not then believe?" (The Prophets, XXI, 30).

With regard to Muslim dogma, and taking into account the explicit dictates on hygiene in Islam, water is present at the beginning of most rituals of sanctification or purification.

Within this symbolic whole which is as much a matter of regional mythology as allegiance to founding fathers, the sacred water of Zamzam, the

source of which is situated in the courtyard of the Hijr, at the foot of the Kaaba, is one of the elements which most impresses the pilgrim.

Ibn Battuta (1304–1377), the geographer and traveller from Tangiers, reports a belief of the Meccans of his time, according to which the water of Zamzam miraculously augments and swells, every night from Thursday to Friday.[1]

Muslim historiography suggests that the fountain of Zamzam surged up at the feet of Ishmael, the oldest son of Abraham, when his mother, Hagar, was desperately searching for water between two hillocks next to the Kaaba, Safa and Marwa. According to the great Arab historian Tabari (838–923), Ishmael himself unleashed the miracle: "Ishmael began to cry, as children do when they are left alone without their mothers, and having stamped his heel on the ground, again as children do, a spring appeared under his heel."[2]

Finally, one should recall the majestic power of the quartet of the rivers Kawthar, Salsabil, Euphrates and Nile. The two former, called "internal rivers", are in paradise. The Euphrates and the Nile are called "external rivers". The Euphrates flows through Iraq where it forms a vast delta with the Tigris in the Persian Gulf. The Nile is a huge river, the longest in the world (4187 miles). It

The water for ablutions is an essential element which validates prayers.

flows through Kenya, Rwanda, Burundi, the Congo, Ethiopia, the Sudan and Egypt, into the Mediterranean. From ancient times (as mentioned by Plutarch), until the construction of the Aswan Dam (opened in 1971), its rate of flow was particularly devastating for Egyptian agriculture and sometimes for the inhabitants themselves.

The Muslim paradise, a vast verdant garden, contains the Kawthar and the Salsabil, two rivers mentioned in the Qur'an, but there also flow rivers of milk, wine, honey and water: "(Here is) a Parable of the garden which the righteous are promised: In it are rivers of water incorruptible; rivers of milk of which the taste never changes; rivers of wine, a joy to those who drink; and rivers of honey pure and clear. In it there are for them all kinds of fruits; and grace from their Lord..." (Muhammad, XLVII, 15).

There are also gushing fountains for the refreshment of the Chosen Ones who abide in paradise. Finally, however idyllic it already is, this picture would be incomplete without evocations of greenery, oases, receptacles full of water and silver goblets in which flows rare and sealed wine. The blessing imparted by water is both immediate (water keeps the camel driver alive in the desert) and complex (water is at once cleansing, beneficial and regenerating). Water, when opposed to fire, and sometimes to earth, represents the coldest part of human nature, according to Western medieval medical theory, but it is unlikely that Islam should have been aware of this dimension, conversely favouring its surging movement and dynamism.

Symbol of cleanliness and purification, water is a blessed element.

Does it not also symbolise nature regenerated, the divine omnipotence, the compassion of Allah? This is made all the more clear in the sura entitled Al-Nûr, which testifies: "Allah has created every animal from water" (The Light, XXIV, 45).

1. Ibn Battuta, *Voyages*, vol. 1, p. 319.
2. Tabari, *Chronique traditionnelle*, vol. 1, p. 164. (Paris: Sindbad, 1980).

CHAPTER 22

COLOURS

ALL COLOURS ARE RESPECTED IN ISLAM. SOME, SUCH AS GREEN, ARE GIVEN GREATER IMPORTANCE

GREEN IS THE COLOUR OF ISLAM, SINCE GREEN WAS FIRSTLY THE COLOUR OF THE BANNER OF THE PROPHET AND OF THE ROBE OF 'ALI (d. 661), the fourth Caliph of Islam. Since then, the Prophet's descendants (*sharif*) have considered green as the mark of their reign, the colour being one of the links, however indirect, with the Prophetic period.

In daily life, green plays a part which confirms and reinforces a symbolic significance gained over the course of time. In Syria, it is said of a person who has the *baraka* that they have a "green hand". This person is a good omen.

The symbol of springtime renewal, another sign of life, green is the colour of joy, success and happiness. Arabic has an extensive vocabulary for the different shades of green. It flourishes in the Qur'an, permeates the language of theology and is as essential in literature as in classical poetry. Finally, a significant number of professions—dyeing, decoration, illumination, chemistry, botany, horticulture and agriculture—accord it particular prominence. Even if there is no real link with the Creator, green is so revered that some very pious Muslims hesitate to pray on a green carpet for fear of offending Islam.

On the contrary, in order to express faith and attachment to the teachings, and since green symbolises hope and peace, mosques, catafalques, house interiors and royal, tribal and family emblems are often painted green.

Finally, the domination of green in heraldic symbolism and in the content of national flags is well known. Examples include the Kingdom of Saudi Arabia, Libya, Pakistan, the Comoro Islands and Mauritania. It also figures prominently in numerous other flags: the Sherif's star on the Moroccan flag, the horizontal or vertical stripes on the flags of Algeria, Kuwait, Jordan, Iraq, Iran, etc.

There are several other colours which, like green, convey a particular symbolism or sign of belonging.

The colour black acquired an importance which has lasted for centuries, when it was adopted by the Abbassid dynasty, which was established in Baghdad at the end of the eighth century. In ancient Persia (now Iran), black represented the devil, while yellow was the colour of mourning and sometimes jealousy. Nowadays, the robes of mullahs are either black or white, or both. Since the death of the Imam Hussein, at the infamous battle of Karbala' in 680, black, the mark of mourning, has become the symbol of Shi'ism as a whole and its clergy in particular. The signifi-

Green is very prominent in Muslim countries and is the colour which has the most symbolic meanings.

cance of the black veil of the Iranians, the *chador*, is related to this context.

White—the colour of the shroud, of angels, etc.—is a complex colour for Muslims. It is the colour of the grand sheikh's *gandura* and of the student's *qamis* (long tunic), but also of the funerary winding-sheet. However, if one goes by a *hadith* of the Prophet: "God loves white clothing, and He has made paradise white", it can be seen that white is a predominantly positive colour in Islam.

In North Africa and Egypt, earth colours prevail although green and white still symbolise noble or abstract sentiments. The *kashabia* of the Algerian high plateaux is brown or dark, while around the Algerian city of Constantine the veil is black.

In the time of Andalusian Spain, red, the colour of fire and blood, the colour of passion, dominated in clothing, as can still be seen in the costume of the flamenco dancer. Today red is still found in the most wide-ranging domains, especially in folklore and traditional dress. Furthermore, the national flags of several Muslim countries are dominated by red: Tunisia, Indonesia, Morocco and Turkey. In this last case, red recalls the Ottoman origins (thirteenth to twentieth centuries) of the national flag. Finally, red figures on other flags, in particular those which, to a greater or lesser degree, are drawn from the four colours of pan-Arabism (red, white, black and green), such as Palestine, Egypt, Iraq and Syria, but also the Sudan, Yemen, and so on.

Muslims perceive the hereafter in terms of colour. Paradise itself, apart from the white mentioned above, has a wealth of other colours. These are evoked in an abundance of silks, delectable beverages and the murmur of water. On the subject of the Chosen Ones, the Qur'an writes: "They will be adorned [...] with bracelets of gold, and they will wear green garments of fine silk and heavy brocade; they will recline therein on raised thrones" (The Cave, XVIII, 31). In the sura Al-Insan, it is also written: "Upon them will be seen green garments of fine silk and heavy brocade" (Man, LXXVI, 21).

The Islamic field of colours, dominated by the peaceful, joyous colour green, is intended as a response adapted to the Muslim's aspirations to calm and serenity.

Opposite: Detail of a dress embroidered in green silk on a background of ruby red. Bengal, nineteenth century.
Following double page: Calligraphy of Allah and Muhammad, from a religious manuscript. Turkey,
Ottoman art, early nineteenth century. Galerie J. Soustiel.

CONCLUSION

Physical symbolism is not that which best charac-terises Islam. This is a religion which relies less on the accumulation of material objects for ritual use than most other religions, and more on abstract representation. Islam professes abstraction and emphasises the strong inner conviction of the believer (*niyya*), a synthesis of will (*irâda*), obedi-ence (*tâ'a*) and freedom (*huriya*).

On the other hand, the life of the community is more characteristic of Islam. As a monotheistic religion of equality, Islam implies universal partic-ipation in communal acts of rallying or assem-bling. The profession of faith, prayer, almsgiving, the fast and pilgrimage, the five canonical duties, are the most prominent expressions of a believer's adherence to his faith.

Faith necessitates a continuous deepening through immersion in, and meditation and the reading of the revealed texts. On a day to day level, Islam is a true religion of "living together", which precludes individual striving, the life of the cloister and the vow of chastity. Celibacy is frowned upon because of the Prophet's own encouragement of Muslims to marry. In the same way, monasticism does not exist, and vows of silence are prohibited. Indeed, a solitary quest for a possible confirmation of faith can only be doomed to failure. Everything is done communally: donation, fasting, charity, pilgrimage, the weekly prayer, secular festivities, circumcision, marriage and the *mussim* (meetings of a religious nature).

While the Qur'an may not expressly have forbid-den the representation of the human form, tradition, by long eschewing it, has rendered it impracticable. The representation of God and His Prophet has therefore always been deemed heretical.

Surely miniatures (*al-munamnama*), however, are the true paintings of the Indo-Persian culture? This is an elegant, refined art which, throughout the centuries, especially in the classical period of Indian, Turkic and Iranian art (fifteenth to sixteenth cen-turies), has always conferred its letters patent of nobility without to any extent diminishing the con-viction of the Muslims. The question could also be asked as to whether calligraphy, mosaics and archi-tecture do not hold the position of sacred art in Islam. Are not these art forms which gratify the curiosity of the person racked with doubt while at the same time soothing him?

All these interpretations are possible, since all are part of the fundamental logic of Islam which states that striving to understand is to be preferred above all things, including closed dogma, as long as it is nourished by beauty.

GLOSSARY

'ADA: custom, ancestral practice

ADHÂN: call to prayer, hence *mu'adhdhîn (muezzin)*

AHL AL-KITAB: the "People of the Book", essentially Jews and Christians

'ALÎM, pl. **'ULAMA:** scholars, college of theologians

Allah: name of the Muslim God

ALLAHU AKBAR: God is (the) Most Great

ALMORAVIDS: an Arabian-Berber dynasty in North Africa (eleventh century)

AMIR: origin of the word *emir*, war lord, governor of a province

'ANSARS: "Auxiliaries", the Medinan partisans of the Prophet

ARKÂN: pillars, foundations; the five Pillars: *al-arkân al-khams*

'ASHURA: tenth day of *Moharram*, the first month of the Islamic year

AYA: Qur'anic verse

AYATU'LLAH: sign of Allah, the title of the Shi'i high dignitary

BARAKA: blessing

BASMALA: name of the inaugural formula of Islam

BAYT ALLAH: the House of God, the Kaaba, Mecca

BID'À: blameworthy, heretical innovation

CALIPH, from the Arabic **KHALIF:** successor, replacement, sovereign

DAR AL-HARB: the Abode of War

DAR AL-ISLAM: the Abode of Islam

DA'WA: preaching

DHIKR or **ZIKR:** mystical prayer

DU'À: personal invocation to God (as distinct from prayer)

FAQIH, pl. **FUQAHA:** person with authority stemming from his religious knowledge (*fiqh*)

GHUSL: major ablutions, washing

HADITH: words, sayings or stories attributed to the Prophet

HAFÎZ, pl. **HUFFÂZ:** person who recites the Qur'an by heart

HAJJ: pilgrimage; hence the title *haji* (fem. *haja*) given to someone who has performed it according to the prescribed rules

HAJR AL-ASWAD: "Black Stone"

HALAL: licit, particularly with regard to food

HARAM: Forbidden (space), especially Mecca and its immediate surroundings

HIJAB: woman's veil, also called *litham, chador, chadri*, etc.

HIJRA: exodus, banishment, beginning of the Muslim era

HILAL: crescent moon

I'JÂZ: inimitable nature of the Qur'an

IMAM: the person who stands in front of the first row of Muslims during prayer. By extension: Muslim scholar attached to the mosque

JAHILIA: paganism, the pre-Islamic era

JAMI': great mosque

JIHAD: self-control, but also holy war

JINN: genie, demon

KAABA: "cubic" temple situated in Mecca

KHATIB: preacher, hence *khutba*; preaching, sermon

KHITÂN or **TAHARA:** circumcision

QUR'AN: from *Qu'rân*, reading, recitation, name of the Holy Book of the Muslims

MADHHAB: Sunni theological school, of which there are four: Shafiism, Hanafism, Hanbalism, Malikism

MADRASSA, MEDERSA (MAGHREB) or MEDRESE (TURKEY, IRAN): Qur'anic school, institution where Islamic dogma is taught

MAHDI: the Rightly-Guided One (by God), in Shi'ism the Hidden Imam

MAHOMET: Anglicised name of Muhammad

MAKKA: Mecca

MANARA: minaret

MATAF: the route of *tawaf*, circumambulation of the Kaaba

MAYSIR: games of chance (Qur'anic term)

MIHRAB: prayer niche showing the direction of the *qibla*

MINBAR: preacher's pulpit

MI'RAJ: ascension of the Prophet to heaven

MULLAH: religious authority in Shi'ism

MUJAHID, pl. MUJAHIDIN: fighter in the path of God

MUFTI: *Qadi* or *Imam* who can issue a religious announcement (*fatwa*)

MUHAJIRUN: the partisans of the Prophet Muhammad

MUTAWIF: attendant during *tawaf*, the rite of circumambulation

NIYYA: good intention. Required as a preliminary to every ritual act

QADI: religious judge or theologian well-versed in matters of law

QIBLA: direction of the Kaaba (Mecca)

QUREYSH: name of the tribe of the Prophet, hence the title *Qureyshite*

RAMADAN: name of the month of lawful fasting

RAQ'A: unit of prayer

RIBA: usury

SADAQA: alms, charity

SAFA and MARWA: two of the sites visited by pilgrims in Mecca

SALAT: canonical prayer, hence *musalla* (place of prayer)

SAWM: fast

SEFEVID: sixteenth-century Iranian dynasty

SHAFIISM: one of the four theological schools of Sunnism

SHAHADA: profession of faith

SHARI'A: religious law

SHARIF or SHERIF: nobleman, descendant of the Prophet

SHAYTAN: Satan

SHI'ISM: second largest branch of orthodox Islam after Sunnism

SIRA: biography of the Prophet

SUFI: mystic

SUFISM: mysticism

SUJUD: kneeling

SUNNA: tradition, the "Traced Path" of the Prophet and his Companions. Origin of the word Sunnism, the most important branch of Islam. It is composed of three parts: *sunna qawliya* (words), *sunna fi'liya* (acts) and *sunna taqrirya* (approbation and participation)

SURA, pl. SURAT: chapter of the Qur'an

TA'WIL: explanation, interpretation of the Qur'an

TAYAMMUM: authorised dry ablutions

TURBE: mausoleum (Turkish)

WUDU': ablutions

ZAKAT: legal almsgiving equivalent to a tax

ZAMZAM: well situated in the heart of the great mosque (Mecca)

ZIKR or DHIKR: mystic prayer

BIBLIOGRAPHY

AL-GHAZALI, *Ihya 'Ulum ed-Din* (Vivification of the Science of the Faith), 4 vols. Cairo, 1933.

AL-QAYRAWANI (Ibn Abi Ziyad), *La Risala ou Épître sur les éléments du dogme et de la li de l'islam selon le rite malikite*, translated into French by L. Bercher. Algiers: Editions populaires de l'armée, 1975.

AL-QUARADAWI, Y., *The Lawful and the Prohibited in Islam.* London: Sharouk International, 1985.

ARBERRY, A. J., *Muslim Saints and Mystics.* London: Routledge and Kegan Paul, 1966.

ARKOUN, M., *Essais sur la pensée islamique.* Paris: Maisonneuve et Larose, 1984.

BOSWORTH, C. E., *The Islamic Dynasties.* Edinburgh: Edinburgh University Press, 1980.

BOUAMRANE, Ch., GARDET, L., *Panorama de la pensée musulmane.* Paris: Sindbad, 1984.

BOUSQUET, G.-H., *Les Grandes Pratiques rituelles de l'islam.* Paris: PUF, 1949.

BROCKELMANN, C., *History of the Islamic Peoples.* London: Routledge and Kegan Paul, 1982.

BURCKHARDT, T., *Art of Islam: language and meaning*, translated by J. Peter Hobson. London: World of Islam Festival, 1976.

DERMENGHEM, E., *Le Culte des saints dans l'islam maghrébin.* Paris: Gallimard, 1954.

DESVERGERS, N., *Arabie*, Paris: F. Didot Frères, 1847.

DONALDSON, D. M., *The Shi'ite Religion.* London: Luzac and Company, 1933.

EL-BOKHARI (Ibn Ismail al-Bukhari), *Les Traditions islamiques*, 4 vols. Paris: Adrien Maisonneuve, 1984.

ENCYCLOPAEDIA OF ISLAM, edited by H.A.R. Gibb et al., new edition, 8 vols. Leiden: E.J. Brill, c. 1986.

GARDET, L., ANAWATI, M.-M., *Introduction à la théologie musulmane.* Paris: J. Vrin, 1981.

GAUDEFROY-DEMOMBYNES, M., *Mahomet.* Paris: Albin Michel, 1969.

———. *Muslim Institutions.* London: George Allen and Unwin, 1950.

GLASSÉ, C., *The Concise Encyclopedia of Islam.* New York: HarperCollins, 1991.

GOLDZIHER, I., *Le Dogme et la loi de l'islam.* Paris: Paul Geuthner, 1973.

GRABAR, O., *The Formation of Islamic Art.* New Haven: Yale University Press, 1973.

HAMIDULLAH, M., *Les Pèlerinages de l'islam.* Paris: Seuil, 1950.

IBN 'ARABI, *La Sagesse des prophètes.* Paris: Albin Michel, 1974.

IBN 'ATA ALLAH, *Traité sur le nom d'Allah.* Paris: Les Deux Océans, 1981.

IBN BATTUTA, *Voyages*, translated into French by C. Defremery and R. Sanguinetti (1858), 3 vols. Paris: La Découverte, 1982.

———. *Travels in Asia and Africa, 1325–1334*, translated and selected by H.A.R. Gibb. New York: A.M. Kelley, 1969.

IBN HISHAM, *The Life of Muhammad*, translated by A. Guillaume. Karachi: Oxford University Press, 1970.

IBN JUBAYR, *Voyages*, translated into French by Gaudefroy-Demombynes, 3 vols. Paris: Paul Geuthner, 1953–56.

IBN KHALDUN, *The Muqaddimah; an introduction to history*, translated by Franz Rosenthal, 3 vols. New York: Pantheon Books, 1958.

IMAM SHAFI'I, *Mousnad.* Paris: Dâr At-Tassili, 1989.

LINGS, M., *Muhammad.* London: George Allen and Unwin, Islamic Texts Society, 1983.

MASSIGNON, L., *Al-Hallaj, Martyr mystique de l'islam*, 4 vols. Paris: Gallimard, 1975.

NAWAWI, *Les Quarante Hadiths.* Paris: Les Deux Océans, 1980.

PAREJA, F. M., HERTLING, L., BAUSANI, A., BOIS, Th., *Islamologie.* Beirut: Imprimerie catholique, 1957–1963.

PENRICE, J., *A Dictionary and Glossary of the Koran.* London: Curzon Press, 1970.

QUR'AN. *The Meaning of the Holy Qur'an* by 'Abdullah Yusuf 'Ali. Amana Publications, 1995.

RAZI, F. ad.-D., *Traité sur les noms divins*, translated into French by M. Gloton, 2 vols. Paris: Devry Livres, 1986–1988.

SCHACHT, J., BOSWORTH C. E., *The Legacy of Islam.* Oxford: The Clarendon Press, 1974.

SOURDEL, D. and J., *Dictionnaire historique de l'islam.* Paris: PUF, 1996.

TABARI, *Chronique traditionnelle*, translated into French by H. Zotenberg, 6 vols. Paris: Sindbad, 1980.

TABARI, *Ta'rikh al-rusul wa-al-muluk (The History of al-Tabari)*, 38 vols. Albany, N.Y.: State University of New York Press, c. 1987.

WATT, W. M., *Islamic Philosophy and Theology.* Edinburgh: Edinburgh University Press, 1962.

———. *Muhammad's Mecca: history in the Qur'an.* Edinburgh: Edinburgh University Press, 1988.

ACKNOWLEDGMENTS

Upon completion of this book, I would like to thank my wife, Samia, my son, Mikail, who will understand one day why I was not always available when he would have liked, and particularly Louahem M'Sabah Mohamed for helping me so frequently and effectively. My thanks are also due to a very dear person who does not wish to be named, but who will recognise himself. Gh. H.-E and Hichem Ben Yaiche read the text while it was still in its embryonic stages, and Hocine Rais, the Director of Cultural Affairs at the Muslim Institute in Paris contributed judicious comments.

Laziz Hamani wishes to thank Philippe Sebirot who greatly contributed to the production of the photographs, and Daniel Delisle at Studio Delisle. Thanks also to Yannis Hamani, Fatima Hamani, Adel Hamani and Cacho Vasquez, who posed for the camera. To Paul Goirand and Florence Moll at Plastic Studio. To Martine and Prosper Assouline, who allowed all these images to be created.

The editor wishes to thank M. Soustiel and Mme David from the Galerie J. Soustiel, whose immense kindness and invaluable collaboration were a great support in the completion of this work. Thanks also to Mme Fegali of the Embassy of Saudi Arabia in Paris, to Nahla Nassar from the Nour Foundation, the Nasser D. Khalili Collection of Islamic Art, to Bernard Huchet and Alain Dovifat.

Our joint thanks go to the Paris Mosque, which helped us in the creation of this book and most particularly to Dalil Boubakeur and Said Bakiri.